Tom Finnigan

Belfast 2024.

ESSAYS BY DIVERS HANDS:
INNOVATION IN CONTEMPORARY LITERATURE

BEING THE TRANSACTIONS OF THE
ROYAL SOCIETY OF LITERATURE

New Series: Volume XL

ESSAYS BY DIVERS HANDS: INNOVATION IN CONTEMPORARY LITERATURE

*being the transactions of
the Royal Society of Literature,
New Series: Volume XL*

EDITED BY VINCENT CRONIN, FRSL

*Published for
the Royal Society of Literature
by the Boydell Press*

© *1979 Contributors*

First published 1979 by The Boydell Press,
an imprint of Boydell & Brewer Ltd, PO Box 9,
Woodbridge, Suffolk IP12 3DF

British Library Cataloguing in Publication Data
Essays by divers hands. New series
Vol. 40
1. English literature – History and criticism
I. Cronin, Vincent   II. Royal Society of
Literature
820′.9   PR13
ISBN 0–85115–119–1

Printed in Great Britain by
Fletcher & Son Ltd, Norwich

CONTENTS

INTRODUCTION

The present volume of *Essays by Divers Hands*, unlike those in the past, treats a single theme: Innovation in Contemporary Literature. In our letter of invitation we asked contributors—all of them writers—to 'talk about one or more of the ways in which they have tried to break new ground or apply new techniques'. We asked that the talks should be personal, and record intentions that failed as well as definite achievements. We hoped that they would throw light not only on the writer's own literary problems but on those faced by other writers of our age.

We expected, and got, diversity of approach. Some lecturers even disclaimed any innovatory character for their books, but in the end all the lectures revealed, explicitly or implicitly, the spirit that extends frontiers.

Seamus Heaney flew from Ireland to give the first lecture. His warm, undulating poet's voice and Ulster accent added to our pleasure as we listened to him tell how he transmutes feelings into words. Particularly interesting was how a chance-seen photograph of the skull of a strangled Iron Age woman in Jutland came to provide the needed image for his emotion at recent tragic killings in Ireland.

The skull as an image reappeared in the lecture given by Charles Tomlinson. Tomlinson is a painter as well as a poet and he spoke about the mutual influence of the two art forms. He told us how drawing the skull of a cormorant picked up on a beach made him aware of its hidden, mysterious aspects, and these, re-sistant to his pencil, built up and outwards to become a poem about the skull.

The novelist Thomas Hinde bravely tackled innovation both of subject and technique. He explained how he came to choose drug-taking for his novel *High*, and how he solved to his own satisfaction the conflict between his pressing American material and his determination not to use it in the way it had been used all too often.

Literary self-analysis has severe limitations and some blind spots, but it can offer unique inside information about a work, sometimes of a kind too odd or irrational to be proposed seriously by a critic. This emerged in several of the lectures, including the one which William Sansom, a few months before his untimely death, gave to short-story writing. Sansom confessed to having a visual mind and an ability to paint. So before embarking on a story he had to be able to picture his characters and his first scene down to the smallest detail of shape and colour. He then gave us insight into the process of plotting by describing how his story 'Cops and Robber' originated in glimpses of some very odd happenings indeed near his London home. As a later lecturer reminded us, William Sansom's declared hobby was Watching—but always with a humorous gleam in his eye.

The writing of biography was discussed by Robert Gittings. Biography, he claimed, is a genre which has come of age in the second half of this century. It has grown multi-dimensional. This makes increased demands on the biographer, who cannot afford to neglect any clue, however tiny, to his subject's tastes, and hence to his values. Biographers in the audience felt sympathy for Dr Gittings as he described the strong resistance he had met from the public when trying to free Keats and Hardy from certain hoary but tenacious legends.

John Stewart Collis, who possesses Blake's gift of seeing a world in a grain of sand, spoke about a subject he has made peculiarly his own: natural philosophy. He let us into the secret of how he transmutes ordinary things—a drop of water or a lump of coal—into extraordinary, even miraculous beauties—by weighting *élan* with homely, down-to-earth detail.

Ronald Blythe emphasized the importance to him of listening. Dialogue, he holds, is one of the surest ways of creating social atmosphere, and as a master of the genre he exemplified Thomas Creevey, contrasting the authentic dialogue of Creevey's Diary with the conventionalized dialogue used by Mrs Creevey in letters to her husband.

Jane Gardam, who has an acute ear for dialogue, spoke to the Society about writing for children. She was candid about her dislike of the Christopher Robins of this, or any, world. As her own children's books show, her preference is for very quick children, not at all given to day-dreaming, eager to discover the weak points as well as the strong in the grown-ups around them, and who can be on occasion self-willed, cruel, even ruthless. Her talk was a refreshing plea for realism even in fairyland.

The doyen of our lecturers, Dr Nirad Chaudhuri, was also the jauntiest. Occasionally almost dancing at the pleasure he seemed to get from lecturing to us, this small man of over eighty delighted in pulling the tails of some of our sacredest cows, including the respect we accord—or used to accord—*A Passage to India*. Dr Chaudhuri demands a political stance from his novelists, and he would rank Rudyard Kipling's books as the best writing by an Englishman about the subcontinent. Since Dr Chaudhuri is himself almost an adopted Englishman, I would suggest that his own book about his native Bengal, *An Autobiography of an Unknown Indian*, qualifies for a place very close to the Kipling he so esteems.

Paul Jennings lectured about Humorous Writing. Since humour and a sense of humour play a greater part in English literature than in any other known to me, the subject is important, and Paul Jennings made it even more so by looking at it, amid his jesting, metaphysically. His contention was that in a world increasingly mechanized and with only a residual belief in God, our one remaining absolute—and how we cling to it!—is humour. It is a stimulating thesis, argued with wit and persuasiveness, and if true helps to illuminate twilight areas in their creative processes hinted at by other lecturers, such as William Sansom.

The most valuable result of this series has been, I think, that almost every contributor describes from personal experience at least one aspect of the psychology of innovating. It may be how he rejects certain aspects of the past, how he prepares himself to collect material, how he actually singles out an incident, an image, or how he shapes it. We who listened to the lectures or read them in the pages that follow learn a little of what may be termed the embryology of literature.

VINCENT CRONIN

THE WRITER AS LISTENER

RONALD BLYTHE, FRSL

Read 22 February 1979:
John Guest, FRSL, in the Chair

I T was William Sansom who used to give 'Watching' as his hobby in *Who's Who* and it is true that writers are as watchful as cats. But what of listening? Or is listening an integral part of watching? If it is, then for the purpose of having the privilege to speak to you tonight I would like to isolate listening from the writer's general function of obsessant observation and ask, do we, as poets, novelists and historians, ever attempt to examine or assess our own individual ear? Have we any idea of the range of our listening or of its selectivity? We know that we have long since become quite unashamed about our eavesdropping and we know that there is a subtle difference between what we set out to hear for the purposes of literature, and what we hear involuntarily. We even accept that, like Milton's Comus, there are times when we are all ear in order to take in strains that might create a soul, and when we are especially alert to any passing voice which might suggest a new character. But what we do not know is the extent and pattern of our listening generally. It seems easier to describe what we normally *see* than what we normally hear. Even in the physical sense we allow the eye ranges and limitations which, unless we suffer from very considerable loss of hearing, we deny to the ear. Yet it is likely that the solitary nature of the act of writing, and the accumulative quiet in which most of us spend our working lives, affect our listening capacity, intensifying it in some, distorting it in others. In the long run, of course, the only people who can tell us what we hear are our readers. Our veracity is proved this way for, as Thoreau said, 'It takes two to speak the truth, one to speak, and another to hear.'

Listening in the strict sense of the word means to hear attentively. Yet literature abounds with remarkable things which the writer heard because he was *not* paying this kind of classroom attention, and by this I do not mean inner voices and the like, but actual sounds, usually sentences, floatingly acquired. Those speaking these sentences, did they but know that they were being so effortlessly intercepted, could say, 'I am not talking to *you*!' But as every writer knows at such a moment, they are!—and in rivetting tones. His thoughts build up around these syllables which he could have missed had he been listening 'attentively' and his creativity comes into play. Or he might tell himself, 'That's it! I have heard the voice of this decade, or of my time; I have caught its cadence and I can hear how we speak *now*.'

Havelock Ellis in his beautiful essays, *From Rousseau To Proust*, a book which led me to French novels and poetry when I was a boy but which, I fancy, is pretty unknown now, wrote, 'When we are young we do not immediately know where we shall hear those voices of our own time to which our virginal hearts will deeply and instinctively respond. They must come from figures of our own time, older than we are or they would not have found expression, but not old enough to have "arrived".' Thus, even if we write into old age, which we should (for there is a rich language which can only be heard then and which needs to be put down) it is important to read young writers of promise. For it is usually only they who can authenticate the present, who can convey its tone.

Attentive, as opposed to unconscious, listening by a writer demands the close hearing of someone else's story for the sake of the story which *he* has to tell. Although for various reasons he may wish to, he will not be able to hear such a story with detachment. Everything from his critical fascination with the narrative itself to the emotion of hearing from another's lips some confession or incident either long withheld or, until now, thought too uninteresting to describe, connects him to the speaker. Such emotion is equal in the force of its impact, even if varied in its origins, should the story come from a father, a friend or a stranger. Each individual speaker in the telling of it will unmask a little, and will add something to the writer's file on human variety and mystery. A man telling one how he makes a wheel—or a fortune—will inadvertently tell one much more. The main thing here is whether the writer possesses a context for what he is being told or whether it is completely out of his academic or social range. The listening writer is frequently drawn back to the voices of his childhood because he knows that they are saying things about his maturity which he will never hear elsewhere. Unlike many a professional interviewer, he finds the guardedness of those he listens to as rewarding as their frankness, for as was said of Proust, 'the power of observation only develops highly in the individual who has a personality to defend'. People can be as reticent about their aspirations as about their crimes, yet one is often struck by the precision and liveliness which accompanies some confessed longing. 'To tell one's dreams one must be infinitely awake,' wrote Paul Valéry, and fantasy is apt to make its owner exceedingly alert. The writer as listener rarely needs the whole tale, and the storyteller often sees little or nothing in what he has to offer, but, as Racine remarked when he had to reply to critical complaint about the emptiness of his *Bérénice*, 'All creation is out of nothing and what God on the seventh day saw as very good, for an unseeing eye (or unhearing ear) it would have still been nothing.' We can repeat Christ's pun after he had told his simple harvest tale about the ears of corn. 'Ye that have ears to *hear*, let him hear.'

Listening was until very recently a somewhat fugitive occupation for the writer. Whether he held what he had heard in his head until diary-time, as Boswell and others did, or whether he took it all down in immediate shorthand, there could be no actual repetition of a story which contained those rests and rushes which created its first impact. But now the writer as listener can hear the original talk on tape—hear it over and over again, pick over its contents and its semantics at his leisure, and could, not only reduce what he once heard with his creative ear to an automatic strip of information, but be in danger of losing the ear itself. Would Boswell have used tape?—had it been invented, that is. No, because the doctor would not have let him. Who should use it? Chiefly those imaginative and creative writers who regard it as an advance on shorthand notes for the collecting of basic information, and oral historians with their philological skills. However, words are words, and the disembodied voice in the writer's study can resurrect a face, a gesture, an attitude, and before he knows where he is his special intelligence is at work, and he is telling us what *he* specifically heard.

I suppose that this process could come under the general title of my lecture—'Innovation in Literature'. When I wrote *Akenfield* I attempted to over-hear what had been said in and around my family for close on a rural century, using neighbourly surrogates for those whom death had silenced. It did not strike me as being innovatory at the time—just a method allowing both them and myself to speak. I remember when I began, and in great trepidation, never having done anything remotely like it before, trying it out on the dog, so to speak, or old Len, whom I had seen since a child. And then, after he had said his piece, as he called it, the shock and humiliation at discovering that I had never 'seen' him and never 'heard' him—not once in all my life. What I had heard and seen was a stocky little outline in the local fields, not this lucid rural intelligence with one foot caught in Cobbett's world and the other capable of finding a purchase in that of the E.E.C., had he lived long enough. From that day on I have regarded even the most open, colourful or predictable people as merely displaying the tip of the iceberg where their full reality is concerned. Not that most writers can hope to discover much more than a fraction of such a reality, yet, by listening to a particularly individual pattern of words, catching a tell-tale emphasis, or recognizing that something is being said which the speaker may not ever have been able to say before, there is a recognition of the infinite possibilities and experiences lying just under the surface of things.

A striking description of what could happen to a writer who is completely cut off from human voices occurs in Michel Tournier's *Friday, Or the Other Island*. This vivid novel, like Jean Rhys's *The Wide Sargasso Sea*, offers an audacious sequel to a previous work of genius, in this case *Robinson Crusoe*. Robinson, as Michel Tournier calls him, does not think of himself as writer but the brilliant extracts from the Journal he is allowed to keep convinces the reader that he is one. But, until Friday appears, Robinson's ears ache for spoken words; without them he realizes that he is being diminished, gradually squeezed of response and literary interpretation.

'I know now,' writes Robinson on his silent island, 'that every man carries within himself—and as it were above himself—a fragile and complex framework of habits, responses, reflexes, preoccupations, dreams and associations, formed and constantly transformed by perpetual contact with his fellows . . . My fellow men were the mainstay of my world . . . Each day I measure my debt to them by observing the fresh cracks in my personal structure. I know what I would suffer should I lose the use of words . . . (Here) there is only one viewpoint, my own, deprived of all context . . . Language in a fundamental manner evoked the *peopled* world, where other men are like so many lamps casting a glow of light around them within which everything is, if not known, at least knowable. Those lights have vanished from my consciousness . . . Since I have been here I have become something of a specialist in silence, or in silences, as I should say. With my whole being intent like a single ear I note the particular quality of the silence at a given moment.' Ironically, when Friday appears he fills Robinson's silences, not with language but with laughter, and directs his listening to what a 'civilized' ear no longer hears, the sensuous clamour of the natural universe. Mystic writers, of course, have their listening habits re-directed in a similar fashion. A further irony which Michel Tournier employs when he forces the reader to contemplate what the wordless effect of a desert island must have on a writer whose ear is instinctively greedy for speech, is to remind us that Robinson Crusoe was brought up in the Quaker religion, a faith which prohibits too much talk. Is it a divine rebuke for his conversation-craving, therefore, that when Robinson does find someone to listen to, he should be a 'savage' and thus in seventeenth-century terms not much advance on a talking dog? How Friday's human voice gradually penetrates an ear which has so long been stuffed-up with written ethics that it has forgotten the spoken give and take of our common humanity, has its lesson for all of us.

Great novelists in particular have always revealed historic movement and social change and transition in a kind of build-up of seemingly casual talk. Immersed in their own artistically contained world, the characters of Sterne, Jane Austen, Flaubert, Thackeray, etc. also tell us about their world at large, though not in so many words. Yet their times are there. In order to convey the ceaseless shifts of society—and thus the ceaseless changes in the texture of its talk—Dickens created a marvellous series of party scenes ranging from the benign (Dingly Dell) to the grotesque (the evening entertainments laid on by Mr and Mrs Veneering and Mr and Mrs Podsnap in *Our Mutual Frind*, masterly cross-currents of solecism as the newly enriched victors of the industrial revolution heave their way into the ranks of the upper bourgeoisie).

Some years ago I was shown the minute-books of the Great Yarmouth Literary Club and was enthralled to discover that now and then both Lord Nelson and Charles Dickens signed as honorary guests. But even more enthralling was the familiar note of jollity and affability sounded by the secretary in his copper-plate hand. It was like voices-off saluting 'Pickwick' or the cosy mumbling from coffee-rooms with closed baize doors. Dickens had not begun to write his comic masterpiece then, but he was all ears at Great Yarmouth. The affability which resounded among the 'bran-new' possessions of Podsnap and Veneering required a very different interpretation—and got it! We laugh now at the dazzling invention and brio of it all, but how it must have lacerated hosts of Dickens's contemporaries as it caught the very accent of their pretensions and their materialism! Much has been said of his night walks in search of copy through London's rookeries but, in another sense, the language he listened to among the rising middle-class of the mid-nineteenth century offered an equal challenge to his genius. Have you noticed how the children of what one might call the talkers-in-transition in *Our Mutual Friend* reveal a different attitude, and often accent, to that of their parents? But although finer, it is less confident. Or, as in Miss Podsnap's reply to Mrs Lammle, it is a decision to shut-up, once and for all. *But*, if Mrs Lammle or anyone else persisted, Miss Podsnap would give her something to talk *about*, though *not* with *her*. (It is one way of crippling a conversation.)

Mrs Lammle was overjoyed to escape into a corner for a little quiet talk.

It promised to be a very quiet talk, for Miss Podsnap replied in a flutter, 'Oh! Indeed, it's very kind of you, but I am afraid I *don't* talk.'

'Let us make a beginning,' said the insinuating Mrs Lammle, with her best smile.

'Oh! I am afraid you'll find me very dull. But Ma talks!'

. . . 'Fond of reading perhaps?'

'Yes. At least I—don't mind that so much . . .'

'M-m-m-m-music.' So insinuating was Mrs Lammle that she got half a dozen m's into the word before she got it out . . .

'Of course you like dancing? . . .'

'Oh no, I don't . . .'

'No? With your youth and attractions? Truly, my dear, you surprise me!'

'I can't say,' observed Miss Podsnap, after hesitating considerably, and stealing several timid looks at Mrs Lammle's carefully arranged face, 'how I might have liked it if I had been a—you won't mention it, *will* you?'

'My dear! Never!'

'No I am sure you won't. I can't say then how I would have liked it, if I had been *a chimney-sweep on May-day*.'

Then we come to Thomas Creevey, listener extraordinary to the Regency, and insatiable recorder. It is now well-nigh impossible for us to understand how it came about that this plump little lawyer from nowhere, socially speaking, was such a hit with his contemporaries, from the Royal family down. Yet it is to him that we are indebted for every cough and rustle of those years. Of course, there are the Greville Memoirs, but Greville's ear had an official tilt to it and was more analogous to that of a Dick Crossman than to the artist in gossip. Mr Creevey had the entrée because he had no fish to fry and because there was virtually nothing too small or insignificant in what another person had to say for it not to engage his undivided attention. He was thus uniquely qualified for being invited everywhere, which he was. Those who will listen with undisguised sympathy and an unprofessional keenness to trifles will be told, on occasion, History with a capital H.

Among Mr Creevey's recordings of the latter, none is more astonishing or impressive than what emerged from his casual encounter with the Duke of Wellington immediately after Waterloo. The Duke, you will remember, had left the battlefield and returned to Brussels after writing half of his dispatch. ('I came back'—that is from another room in the inn at Waterloo where he had visited a wounded friend—'had a cup of tea and some toast, wrote my dispatch, and then rode into Brussels [where] I met Creevey . . . and he called out to me, "*What news?*" '

And that, I think, was the secret of Creevey's success, the triumph of his nature—to possess not only a tongue but a presence which made everyone he met feel that they had news to give. He was all ears to all men. Which is why he became a perpetual guest and welcome everywhere until the day of his death. 'He possesses nothing but his clothes,' wrote Greville. 'He has no home, no servant, no creditors and no ties . . . I think he is the only man I know in society who possesses nothing.' Except the confidences of his age, one should add, a vast ocean of talk channelled into his *Journal* in handwriting so dreadful that it might almost have acted like a code.

But back to one of Mr Creevey's major scoops. The Duke, having won the battle which settled the fate of Europe for the next hundred years, and having had his tea and toast, was standing pensively in his hotel window when who should be staring up at him but Mr Creevey, the very man everyone had to tell everything to, and thus the Duke beckoned, and poured it all out in his 'short, natural, blunt way . . . and without the least approach to anything like triumph or joy'.

' "It has been a damned serious business. Blücher and I have lost 30,000 men. It has been a damned nice thing—the nearest run thing you ever saw in your life . . ." He repeated so often its being *so nice a thing—so nearly run a thing*, that I asked him if the French had fought better than he had ever seen them do before?—"No," he said, "they have always fought the same . . ." Then he said, "By God! I don't think it would have done if I had not been there." '

When Creevey sent the letter containing this talk home (in the same bag as that carrying Wellington's dispatches on his victory), he omitted the last sentence as 'It did not seem fair to the Duke to state it without full explanation, as there was nothing like vanity in the observation in the way he made it.' But when seven years later the Duke became 'very foolishly, in my opinion, a politician', Creevey replaced the sentence. The writer as listener has discovered an area in which talk is rigged, and the talker premeditated and cautious. Creevey's collection of Waterloo talk instances his brilliant selectivity of material for in the midst of this vast drama and its comment—its screams, too, for immediately after the battle he wandered across the field—he heard a military doctor say that the thousands of wounded left there two whole nights stood a better chance of recovery than those unfortunate enough to have been taken to hospital.

Nor can we leave this splendid listener without a word about his wife. Did he recognize in her a similar craving, or did she catch it from him? Or was she his pupil? She was a widow and the mother of six when she married him, and they seemed to have divided their engagement book, with Mrs Creevey covering those dinners and routs which coincided with his, and sending him by way of letters everything she saw and heard. But the listening was different. What is said is a kind of telling fragmentation set in a sparkling narrative, like curls in a locket.

Oh, this wicked Pavilion! we were there till ½ past one this morng., and it has kept me in bed with the headache till 12 today . . . When the Prince appeared, I instantly saw that he had got more wine than usual, and it was still more evident that the German Baron was extremely drunk. The Prince came up and sat by me . . . and talked a great deal about Mrs Fitzherbert . . . Afterwards the Prince led all the party to the table where the maps lie, to see him shoot with an air-gun at a target placed at the end of the room. He did it very skilfully, and wanted all the ladies to attempt it. The girls and I excused ourselves on account of our short sight; but Lady Downshire hit a fiddler in the dining-room, Miss Johnstone a door and Bloomfield the ceiling . . . I soon had enough of this, and retired to the fire with Mac . . . At last a waltz was played by the band, and the Prince offered to waltz with Miss Johnstone, but very quietly, and once round the table made him giddy, so of course it was proper for his partner to be giddy too; but he cruelly thought of supporting himself, so *she* reclined on the Baron.

There is a familiar note in what Mrs Creevey hears and we recognize it—in Thackeray. Mr Creevey cannot achieve this insouciance, this dashing-off of the deplorable. Just a week after this romp she is with the Prince at Brighton Pavilion when: 'Harry Grey has just come in with news of a great victory at sea and poor Nelson being kill'd . . . What will this do? not, I hope, save Pitt . . .' She picks up a conventional sentence or two to illustrate Prinny' grief, which was very real, but she lacks the right antennae for such profound tidings and cannot convey their effect. Her ear is actually corrupted, though comically so, by the chatter into which her marriage to Mr Creevey has hurled her. Moreover, what her husband can accept as the necessary rituals of the great world she, with her womanly commonsense, sees as a charade. Each listens intently but what Mrs Creevey hears is so absurd that only a dashing, throwaway style can fix what she hears on to the page. Together, they form a balanced witness of their age.

Among modern novelists who knew how to hear beneath the conversational surface of life the announcements of inescapable change was the late Paul Scott, a Fellow of our Society and a writer whose importance is only now being recognized. What he heard as a young soldier during the last war in India began a process of major penetration into the rich mysteries of the Anglo-Indian dialogue which has succeeded as no other work of fiction has in showing our imperialism in crisis. As with the nineteenth-century novelists he resembles in scope and mounting detail, Scott's *Raj Quartet* is one of those mines of social and political information which have been made accessible by brilliant storytelling and illumined by authentic conversations between representatives of the two countries about to cut adrift. The books move along with a solid narrational power which is chiefly generated by observation and an interior monologue, but their power seems to derive from scatterings or little bursts of very ordinary speech. Too ordinary, maybe, like that heard by Pinter and Beckett, for any but the extraordinary ear. Like these writers Paul

Scott understands that we proceed colloquially by untidy repeti-
tions. Particularly when we have got something important to say.
We learn all we need to know about Miss Crane the spinster
missionary and her colleague Mr Chaudhuri in one of these little
tumbles of talk. The latter has urged her to step hard on the
accelerator as their car approaches the rioters, but she cannot. To
injure someone, to kill him . . . she cannot.

> 'They weren't going to move, they'd have died. I'm sorry.'
> 'Don't speak,' Mr Chaudhuri said. 'Now leave it to me.
> Don't speak.' He put a hand on her wrist. 'Trust me,' he said.
> 'I know you never have, but trust me now. Do whatever I say.
> *Whatever* I say.'
> She nodded. 'I trust you. I'll do what you say . . . But don't
> run risks. I'm not worth risks. I'm old and it's all gone and I've
> failed . . . If this is where it ends for me, let it end.'
> 'Please, Miss Crane,' he said, 'don't be ridiculous.'

In this flutter of words the novelist makes us hear Miss Crane
personifying the Raj at the moment when it hands over its authority. Although he is dealing with vast events, he is anti-epic in
his account of them. There is a constant element of surprise in all
this. His innovation is to move us profoundly by quietly excellent
though orthodox prose and a dispassionate vision. Had he been a
great journalist I suppose he would have been described as
having his ear to the ground. But his listening was never confined
to this or to any other basic level. In the eloquent lecture which
Paul Scott delivered to this Society a decade or so ago, he spoke
of the 'mood of childish irritation brought on by yet another critical comparison of the novels I write about India and the novel
which E. M. Forster wrote' and of how in the end every word
which Forster heard there became for him the utterly dull 'bou-
oum' or 'Ou-boum' of the Marabar cave. The essential difference
between himself and Forster, he said, was that 'my India made
me talkative, and his stunned him into silence'.
   It is a broad description of how current events affect our current literary responses. Except that in the case of our hearing only
bou-oum or ou-boum, our silence must be short-lived, for the
poet, the novelist and the historian never needs to listen more
creatively than when he suspects that there is a hollow at the
heart of things. What made the void? What drained from it?
What has to flood back into it? To ask such questions isn't to
take the now unfashionable optimistic view but to state the obvi-

ous—that you can't make brick without straw. A few have attempted it in their experimental way and have intrigued us, or outraged us, or taught us a thing or two en route, but the majority of us desire and demand to hear talk that makes us talkative. There never was an age without a voice—however lacking in eloquence the previous age accuses it of being. And it is only by a true—and dispassionate, if you like—hearing of this voice that we can artistically create both the individual speaker and the relentlessly shifting social atmosphere from which he can never escape. There could be desperate results, as with a Mandelbaum, a Sylvia Plath or a Solzhenitsyn.

> '*Oh dreadful is the check, intense the agony*
> *When the ear begins to hear, and the eye begins to see.*'

wrote Emily Brontë in her poem *The Prisoner*, and we with our daily helping of media-conveyed sounds and sights of a mostly suffering world could find it all too much. But when we remember that what we write is a form of self-extension, we know that we cannot reach everywhere and everyone, and that to have defined our personal territory is commonsense.

No great writer in Britain defined his personal territory more absolutely than Thomas Hardy, and none was more personally generous (self-indulgent, some have said) as to what it had to contain. Briefly, it consisted of the social realities of Dorset and the West Country during the first half of the nineteenth century, for his vision was retrospective and, like that of most villagers, ever harking back, plus the reality of his immense literary imagination. Hardy thus heard his own people speaking through his own intricate culture and wrote down what it sounded like. His first reviewers had never heard anything like it in their lives, and said so. R. H. Hutton, reviewing *Far From the Madding Crowd* in the *Spectator* in 1874 said, more in sorrow than in anger, for he admitted that Mr Hardy had a turn for an 'amusing and original story', how much he deplored the author's habit of making an intellectual graft on coarse and vulgar thoughts. 'The reader who has any general acquaintance with the civilization of the Dorsetshire labourer, with his average wages and his average intelligence, will be disposed to say that a more incredible description of them than that which Mr Hardy has given us can hardly be conceived,' and the reviewer particularly distrusts 'the curious flavour of mystical and Biblical transcendentalism' in the rustic talk. How can a servant say to Bathsheba as the field men arrive for their wages, 'The Philistines are upon us!' and what business have labourers to converse in a peculiar style which is deeply infiltrated with this kind of moral irony? Why isn't Mr Hardy like George Eliot, who never confused her own ideas with those of her dramatic figures? Well, to answer all this would involve a long and familiar lecture. I only mention Hardy now because I have been long involved with him during the recent editing of his matchless novels. And also because these old criticisms reminded me of certain criticisms of *Akenfield*. An American reviewer proved my literary infiltration of what had been said by my Suffolk villagers by quoting the last sentence of Len Thompson's talk as an impossible thing for a farmworker to say, that I was a poet and that I had involved Len in my poetry. But Len did in fact say, 'I have these deep lines on my face because I have worked under fierce suns.' It certainly was an odd and untypical remark but it came out of an emotion which our meeting had unwittingly released.

Well, you will say, this talk is supposed to be about innovation in contemporary literature and we have had Creevey and Dickens, and now we have Hardy, but what I am saying, and probably rather obviously, is that the writer's ear, like Prospero's island, is full of noises. The spoken words of his day drift ceaselessly across the words spoken in the myriad, and often haphazardly encountered, books which have brought him his culture. Stories which have *given* him an ear for more stories. We listen to them within the containing bounds of a time and a circumstance but the sentences in them, even when they are blunted clichés, act as litmus as they flare through our imagination, touching off brighter connections, for we are incorrigibly allusive. Yet, for all this, there *is* a language of the hour and whether we are twenty or eighty years old, and whether we like it or despise it, it is always curiously exciting to recognize it. To do so is essential to an understanding of fiction and history particularly, and no one has paid the latter's debt to the language of the hour better than the present Professor of Modern History at Oxford, Richard Cobb, who connects his readers with that of eighteenth-century France as though the simple people speaking it were at the end of the telephone. Cobb says that the historian has much the same assignment as Proust, but as he does not have the advantage of Proust's own memory, he has to construct, then pillage, other people's.

The contemporary novelist and poet, listening to the language of the hour, do not need to construct before they pillage. The words which they are hearing, and which are coming to them with a certain inimitable emphasis simply because it is *Now*, are the expression of a social structure which is all around them. Although, often while standing at bus-stops or in bars, or even in the gallery of the House of Commons, or the home of an old friend, the writer is amazed to hear vivid forms of common speech which are clearly widely used, though not by him. He asks himself, where was I when everybody else was picking it up? Puzzled by the emergence of some new manner of saying things, some not quite definable note in the talk generally which seems to suggest that society has begun to enter one of its soul-searching phases, the writer will return to read books by the reputed spokesmen of his generation, only to discover that, besides being ever so slightly out of date, these spokesmen all arrange current speech in stylish literary patterns which are only joined by the vaguest contemporaneity with the speech he just heard. Or overheard usually, for we are less analytical when we are not eavesdropping. If the altered way of talking persists, as in the clearly different way educated young people talk compared with the educated over forty-fives, a novelist will feel that he must learn the cadence of this speech in order to understand his own times. And so he will make his own patterns of dialogue and monologue, strictly as he hears them, although ignoring the fact that by fixing spoken words to the page we can uplift them or degrade them—or even make them sound as if they had never been in common circulation. Each of us, too, remains faithful to certain 'spokesmen of our time' in the highest literary sense. Whether they warned us or dazzled us, or whether the people in their stories talk in the only way we find acceptable—even now, decades on, they stay part of ourselves.

And so do, though more mysteriously, those audacious masters who seized the strands and inner meanings, the surface glitter and sad heart of communication into their own hands and made what they would of it. Writers like Carroll, Firbank and Ivy Compton Burnett, and those belonging to the experimental school of novelists who developed in the 'sixties, who declared— and often proved—that naturalism is not enough. Some of these have pressed and lobbied for innovation, others have been innovators unawares, and a few have done what they had to do, as they say in a Western film, and have ignored the world's amusement or fury at their mannerisms.

This brings me to the literary respectability of innovation. It has a slightly dubious ring about it which suggests the stretching of a point here or there, or adding gewgaws that catch the eye, or that the writer lacks integrity in dismissing the standard practice and introducing his own. And yet I believe that most of those great innovators (and these include what we call minor writers) who have listened to the talk of their day and then subjected it to their artistry, were never experimentalists. They did not try out some method of literary renewal; they were simply the victims—or victors—of a unique ear which was in perfect collaboration with a unique pen. The novel in particular advances because the new pressures of his day sometimes forces the novelist to express them in a new way. *It is nearly always via dialogue.* If an analysis was made of kaleidoscopic change and development in English writing over the past century—and we must exclude poetry—it would show that nearly all of it related to the treatment of dialogue. Do we hear differently because of all these fluctuating patterns made by spoken words on the page? I think we do. In its best sense, to innovate means to make new, but I think that it is its botanical meaning which is best applied to the writer—the formation of a new shoot at the apex of a stem or branch, especially that which takes place at the apex of the thallus of mosses.

INDIA IN ENGLISH LITERATURE

N. C. CHAUDHURI, FRSL

Read 29 April 1976:
Angus Wilson, CBE, C.Lit., FRSL, in the Chair

I ASSUME that the first thing you are expecting from me is to tell you how the subject of this talk is related to the series: Innovation in Contemporary Literature.

Now, if I wanted to put you off with a flippant answer I could say that a startling innovation is the appearance here of a Babu of the Anglo-Indian demonology. I say demonology advisedly, because to the Englishman in India the word Babu was not simply a colourless label for the Bengali who knew English, but a rune to invoke an unclean presence. I cite the highest authority to substantiate this. In 1913, the year in which a great Babu, Rabindranath Thakur—*anglice* Tagore—brought the Nobel Prize for literature for the second time to Britain following Kipling, the same Kipling wrote to his friend Rider Haggard:

Well, whose fault is it that the Babu is what he is? *We* did it. We began in Macaulay's time: we have worked without intermission for three generations to make this CALIBAN. Every step and thought on the road is directly traceable to England and English influence.

Fair enough, from his point of view. But from the Caliban's I might say that my coming here is a novelty of the same kind, though of course not of the same degree of significance, as St Paul's going up to the Areopagus to proclaim the Unknown God to curious Athenians. And the Unknown God whom you once ignorantly worshipped and whom I declare unto you is the British Empire in India.

But I shall be serious and put forward a plausible justification. Writing about India, ever since its beginnings, has been regarded as a special genre in itself. Moreover, any writing about India in order to be effective has called for many innovations of approach, form, and style. Today, almost a revolution is needed, because, bereft of sincere, secure, and practical moorings in the English mind, writing on India faces a crisis in which truth is in jeopardy.

In the United States it has become virtually impossible to publish any book on India which is authentic unless it is taken up by one of the university presses. By and large, there, India has been delivered over to scribbling charlatans. The position in Britain is not so deplorable, nonetheless it is depressing. As an author who has been publishing here for twenty-five years, I find that, more and more, sound books are being pushed out by the counterfeit, and in any case by trivia. I doubt whether the drift can be checked. However, there is no harm in offering a diagnosis, and by implication a prescription.

But you have the right to ask whether I can be objective. And I assure you that my gloomy appraisal does not arise from personal disappointments.A man who makes out a general case from the starting-point of his own grievances can never speak for truth. He is only a plaintiff, and any truth there might be in his plea has to be discovered by others. I am not in this position.

Actually, I have been exceptionally fortunate in regard to publication in Britain. My books are born within me, and therefore they are like our children whom we leave to the chances offered by the world. I would give the example of my first book, *The Autobiography of an Unknown Indian*, published in 1951. It was an account of the life of a totally unknown Bengali up to his twenty-second year only, and at the formidable length of nearly a quarter of a million words. The life too was remote, strange, and wholly eventless. If any book could be unacceptable to London publishers that one was. Yet it was taken up by one of the foremost, Macmillan, though it had no sponsor.

Furthermore, after publication it was reviewed by the most influential critics. The obscure Indian that I was, still I was the only Indian besides Nehru who had a full-page portrait in the *Illustrated London News*, and it was accompanied by an article by Sir John Squire. My subsequent books, too, have not needed adventitious promotion, and they in their turn have brought me commissions to write other books. This collaboration between my publishers and me is almost as remarkable as the docking of American and Russian spacecraft.

But it was neither planned, nor was it opportunistic. It came about through a spontaneous interest in ideas and feelings, and these were themselves generated by the bombardment of my mind by that great reality India, for which I had become only a medium. This in itself could point to a particular solution of the problem of writing about India. But the relevance or irrelevance of my case to the general situation will not become apparent until I have described that.

To do that I have also to go into its antecedents. In the nineteenth century some interesting fiction, history, and travellers' accounts were published about India, and in addition some minor poetry was also composed. But these were like creeks by the side of a great river. To vary the metaphor, India was an exotic plant in the natural ecology of English letters, and was never acclimatized. This failure has to be accounted for.

The obvious explanation would be that the Indo-British connection was merely political, and therefore could not rouse the kind of emotions which produce literature. But who says that politics cannot inspire great literature? If it were so, the *Iliad*, the *Aeneid*, the *Mahabharata* would not have been written. Besides, if Shakespeare could deal with the Hundred Years' War or Hardy with the Napoleonic there was nothing to prevent a gifted English writer from doing something with Clive, Warren Hastings, or the Mutiny. Ronsard wrote a *Franciade*, and Voltaire an *Henriade* as well as *La Pucelle*.

The real reason behind the minor position of India in English literature was not that the connection was political, but that even politically it was of secondary interest. The deepest emotional involvement of the British people was with fellow-Europeans. Or, not to put too fine a point on it, they rated the killing of fellow-Europeans as a greater national achievement than rescuing a great non-European people from anarchy and oppression and resuscitating their culture. It is this narrowness of the English mind—I would call it racialism in the jargon of today—which has made India go by default in English literature. Is she ever to get her place in it? Not until the current anaemic conception of the Indian Empire is replaced by one which will be true and inspiring.

As it happens, I set down a view which I believe to be the true one only nine months before it came to an end. It was published in November, 1946, in the *New English Review*, edited by Douglas Jerrold and Sir Charles Petrie. In it I said:

> The Empire is no marginal fact of English history, no irrelevant frill, no sowing of wild oats by the exuberant youth of Britain, no dead tumorous growth on an otherwise healthy polity, nor even a preserve of British economic interests . . . It was and remains one of the central facts of universal history and concrete evidence that the British people have discharged one of their primary roles in history. They could not disinterest themselves in it without abrogating their historical mission and eliminating themselves from one of the primary strands of human evolution.

Please remember that this was written in 1946 by a man who was a political suspect under the British regime and whom its political police tried down to 1944 to expel from Government service. And for expressing similar views after independence I am a political suspect in India today.

Of course, the Indian Empire cannot be brought back to enable English writers to establish India in their literature. Even the British ruling class would not say sorrowfully: *Si vieillesse pouvait!* But I wish they could at least say: *Mais vieillesse sait.* Even this they cannot, for the knowledge is disappearing and the feeling for the Empire has sunk very low.

How low, can be judged from the currency of that affected, vulgar, and illiterate word *Raj*. H.M.S. Pinafore could at least be an amusing conceit for H.M.S. Iron Duke of the Grand Fleet, for it would be grammatical. The word *Raj* is not a grammatical formation in any Indian language, ancient or modern. I never heard it employed by anybody, British or Indian, down to 1947. It does not occur in Hobson Jobson. It does not make the Empire so much as a subject of opera buffa, for to write that one needs education. The attitude to the Empire embodied in this tawdry Indianization will not enable India to re-enter English literature.

My emphasis on the political incentive behind literature does not need apology. All the great novelists can be classed either as political or non-political. For example, Stendhal, Dickens, Turgenev or Tolstoy put their stories within a framework of public or collective life, whereas Jane Austen, Balzac, Flaubert, Dostoevsky or Hardy did not. Moreover, novelists today are not the chaste wives of fiction, but have become demi-mondaines, and are half-sociologists. So, giving political settings to Indian stories would be no revolution.

On the contrary, there would be decided advantage, because in the nature of things no foreign writer can gain any inside knowledge of Indian life. They surmount this obstacle by taking up only its marginal expressions. They even invent themes like the impact of a European on a Hindu family, or the sorrows of a young Hindu with a traditional wife foisted on him by his father when after coming to England he meets an English girl with a mind. Nothing happens in either case.

A young Englishman or American who will be received into a Hindu home will already have become such a brainwashed Indophile moron that he will not set any Hindu house on fire. He will either become a tool of Hindu chauvinism or be treated as the family's pet monkey. A white woman will be exploited to satisfy Hindu lust as well as Hindu patriotism.

As to the callow Indian youth who wants a mind in his wife, that too is a myth. The Hindus have been polygamous through the ages, and their outlook even in monogamy is controlled by the old tradition. A polygamist would be the last man to wish for a mind in his wife, for that would make life insupportable. Even a rudimentary mind is a danger. There is a well-known Bengali story in which a man with two wives asks the favourite younger one to pluck off his white hair. The spiteful first wife begins to pull out the black. You who have become crypto-polygamous in these days will readily concede that the mind has very little to do with the assault on monogamy. In actual fact, it is only the monogamous man who cares for a mind in his wife; the polygamous man, as every truthful person will admit, is only after unmentionable parts.

At all events, even though such trivialities can be pot-boiled into novels it is not necessary to go as far afield as India to pick them up. They are plentiful in the glorious multi-racial society you are creating here. But even for treating them a political slant will be better than a purely personal one.

For instance, a novelist who would adopt a girl of the second generation of Indian immigrants as the heroine of a tragedy because of her revolt against marriage with a stranger selected by her father, will soon discover his mistake. He will find that this potential Jane Eyre, this aspirant after self-realization, pronounces the English words *but* as *bott*, *month* as *maunth*, *today* as *todie*, and calls the young yahoo who has taken her fancy for the time being *my lov*. Then he will certainly decide that, instead of being brought into a novel, the creature had better be left in her comprehensive school or be handed over to the Social Service.

On the other hand, by adopting a political stance an English novelist could write a novel in the grand manner. He could show that behind the antipathy to Pakistan and partiality for India in young English dons stand the large black eyes of the girls from Bengal and Madras at Oxford and Cambridge. To these dons these little things are what his flitting soul was to the Emperor Hadrian:

> *Animula, vagula, blandula*
> *Hospes comesque corporis . . .*

And remembering that they will go away as soon as they have taken their degrees the dons sigh—*Eheu, fugaces!*

As a foil, the novelist could show that the resplendent and ampler beauties from the north-western parts of India no longer pull their heavier weight so as to help Pakistan. The reason is that you had the benefit of these beauties without benefit of clergy for a long time, and have lost your taste for them. Here then is an opportunity for an innovation—for playing a variation on a theme by Kipling.

But all this argument is really superfluous. The link between politics and literature in writing about India can be seen by taking a casual glance at the works of Kipling. He is the only Englishman who has succeeded in bringing India into the main stream of English literature, and he did that with a power and brilliance never seen before or since. His is the only writing on India which will remain a permanent part of English literature. I say that in spite of being called Caliban by him.

The magnitude of his achievement can be judged by its worldly aspect alone. In 1907, when Meredith, Hardy, and Bernard Shaw were the leading figures in English letters, it was Kipling who with his Indian writings brought the Nobel Prize for the first time to Britain. Undoubtedly, it was his politics, both true and false, which did the trick.

The importance of politics in securing recognition for writing on India was demonstrated again when in 1924 E. M. Forster brought back the country into English literature with a bang. His *Passage to India* was, if it was anything at all, a political book; in fact, it was rank anti-imperial propaganda. All its novelty lay in that.

However, between Kipling and Forster, there was an intermezzo in which India found a niche in English literature on the strength of the old appeal of her spirituality. That was due to the publication in 1912 of Tagore's *Gitanjali*, a slim volume of translations into English of a number of his religious poems in Bengali, made by himself. The effect was sensational, for it brought the Nobel Prize again to Britain in 1913. Thus Kipling the Anglo-Indian and Tagore the Babu won the prize for Britain long before any English writer could do so. It was only in 1932 that Galsworthy got it. Even he was forestalled by two Irishmen. Thus it can be said that in a worldly way India has brought a spectacular gain to English literature.

But was that also a true literary gain? In Kipling's case there can be no doubt. No writer could have begun to come back in the manner he is doing after falling so low in critical estimation as he did, unless he possessed real greatness. That greatness lies as much in the contents of his writings as in the innovations of form and style he hit upon. To single out just one, he reversed the modern relationship between the roles of poetry and prose by making the first his impromptu expression and the second the vehicle of emotion recollected in tranquillity. This was a reversion to the primitive tradition of poetry.

I would call Kipling great even for that very thing which has brought him obloquy, namely, his imperialism. The Rudyardo Furioso of the meretricious brand of imperialism was not the real imperialist in Kipling. It must not be forgotten that he was not a highly educated man, and that ratiocination was not his strong point. In fact, intellectually he was as hopeless as his cousin Stanley Baldwin. So, in the formation of his opinions he could fall a victim to the shoddy. His genius lay in his acute sense perception and his intuitive insight, combining which he could have the vision of a seer. Thus he could see British rule in India without vainglory as a tragic phenomenon.

The tragedy is felt even in the mood of that much abused poem 'The White Man's Burden'. I am disgusted by the stupidity and hypocrisy of those who denounce it. What I want to know is this: Whether the infatuated belief with which the so-called developed nations are giving thousands of millions of money to the so-called under-developed nations is or is not adherence to the idea of the White Man's Burden. If not, *sacré nom de chien!* what is it? I at least know my mind. As you can see, I am both black and under-developed. But I would a hundred times be called 'Nigger' in your old manner than 'under-developed' in the new. I know very well who take pride in being called under-developed and for what reasons.

At any rate, the Americans for whom Kipling wrote the poem are now coming round. In 1899 he told them:

Take up the White Man's burden—
The savage wars of peace—
Fill full the mouth of Famine
And bid the sickness cease;
And when your goal is nearest
The end for others sought,
Watch Sloth and heathen Folly
Bring all your hope to nought.

At the time this made Boston Brahmins like Charles Eliot
Norton and William James very angry, and their mouthpiece, the
Nation, called Kipling 'a most pernicious vulgar person'. But the
other day the United States put off consideration of aid for India
on account of her anti-American attitude. In explanation, one
Boston Brahmin of today, Moynihan, said that America had been
turning the other cheek too long and should answer back, while
the adopted Boston Brahmin, Kissinger, declared that those who
bite the hand that feeds them should be discouraged from doing
so. But the Americans have yet to learn their full lesson from
Kipling, which is this:

Take up the White Man's burden
And reap his old reward;
The blame of those ye better,
The hate of those ye guard.

You are now coming to think of Solzhenytsyn as a prophet for
egging you on to resume the killing of fellow-Europeans. Suppos-
ing he turns out to be one, I would say that Kipling is already
proved to be one in a bigger, deeper, and more toxic area of
human conflict. But his literary achievement was so interwoven
with British rule in India that he cannot be taken as a model for
any writer on India in the future.

Tagore's example, too, is time-barred. His original appeal was
genuine. Now he is neither read nor admired much. Nevertheless, I would claim a place for him in the corpus of English
poetry on the strength of his renderings from his own poems in
Bengali.

But a correct appraisement of this poetry is not easy to give. As
a writer of religious poetry I would have classed him with the so-
called metaphysical poets of the seventeenth century if it were not
for the extreme naïveté of his English style. This seems to feed
back into the substance of his poetry the same naïveté, and create
the impression that he was one of the popular religious teachers

of India. Most definitely, he was not one of them. His religious sentiment was both complex and profound, it was based on the most abstruse and learned traditions of Hindu religious culture. And in point of technique his poetry was very sophisticated. In English all this disappears.

Comparing his English versions with their Bengali originals, I feel like saying in moments of impatience that the two bear the same relation to each other as the *oggetti religiosi* you can buy on your way to St Peter's do to the sculpture of Chartres. But this would be unfair, because even in the transposition there remains in the pieces an ineffable though tenuous residue of the originals. To describe the attenuated effect I shall give the example of a far-famed touristic attraction of India, namely, the Taj in moonlight. Sir Edwin Lutyens poured ridicule on the sloppiness which could be delighted by the destruction of architectural form, the very essence of architecture. Still, the Taj under the moon can be contemplated as a beautiful wraith of the monument. In the same way Tagore's English versions are tender wraiths of the Bengali poems. But even this cannot be repeated, for Tagore's phantoms had a powerful reality behind them. His religious message is not to be classed with the mush and mumbo-jumbo ladled out by certain writers as Hindu spirituality.

There remains the third personality of the trinity, E. M. Forster. He too is unsuitable as a model for any British writer who wants to write about India, for his novel, *A Passage to India*, with which alone I am concerned in this discussion, is as interwoven with British rule as the stories of Kipling. Furthermore, in spite of the fact that this book is still read and admired, it has to be rated as the worst novel that could have been written about India, and is besides false and malicious.

Many Englishmen, and (curiouser and curiouser) many Americans have quarrelled with me over this opinion. One Englishman has even written that he felt like striking me at a dinner table for disparaging Forster. What marvellous transformations Englishmen are capable of undergoing according to circumstances, without caring how opportunistic they appear! Any literary critic in the Western world who would disagree with me about the merits of *A Passage to India* may please himself. I reconcile myself to the aberration by recalling the tag: *Quem Jupiter vult perdere dementat prius*.

Against all the degenerate partisanship of Forster I will set a massive consensus of opinion. From 1924 to this day I have yet to meet a fellow-Indian whose character and intelligence I respect, who has not been repelled and angered by this novel, though some Indian toadies had *tin kurnish* or the Muslim triple obeisance for him for his condescension. Only the other day a young Muslim told me that he found the book most insulting to Indian self-respect. Why should a wholly uninitiated youth who knows nothing about former Indo-British relations have this feeling? Moreover, every British person with any real knowledge of India, has regarded the book as untrue and malicious.

To expose the faults of this book would require another book. I sum up very briefly. The novel is full of howlers about Indian life which anyone familiar with that life can detect. They destroy all its verisimilitude. All the characters are unreal, as if they were skittles set up to give Forster the satisfaction of knocking them down. As presented, they are all, whether British or Indian, despicable. Above all, in a *roman à thèse* which purports to moralize on Indo-British relations the fundamental assumption is not only wrong but childishly wrong.

Forster's position was this—British rule in India is the cause of so much human maladjustment that on considerations of humanity alone it should come to an end. On the contrary, everyone familiar with British rule in India will tell you that politics did not create the undoubted squalor of Indo-British personal relations, and also that the personal relationship was at its best within the framework of the political relationship, where the consciousness of subjection was most acute. Leaving aside politicians, I have met scores of Bengali revolutionaries who wanted to shoot Englishmen. But from none of them did I hear any language which gave vent to the impotent rancour of Forster's hero. The Muslim Aziz, whom he depicts as an object of compassion, has the spite of a flunkey dismissed for misconduct. He speaks like one. Forster could offer no greater insult to Indian nationalism than by making him its protagonist.

He put this outburst in the mouth of this bounder: 'We shall drive every blasted Englishman into the sea and then you and I shall be friends.' This showed that Forster knew nothing about the nationalist movement, for during its course the Muslims except for a short interlude sided with the British. Even we Hindus did not drive the English into the sea. They themselves chose to plunge into it like lemmings. But that has not made the Indian the friend of the Englishman. If anything, the misunderstanding is worse. Anyone who is not fatuously blind to facts can perceive the new hatred, not only in India, but here in Britain among the Indian immigrants.

I shall leave the book at that. The main question is, however, how Forster came to write that novel. The shortest answer would be that no fruit can be better than the tree. India is a very dangerous country for all Occidentals. A very intelligent French diplomat once told me in Delhi that all Europeans who come to India became either partisan or hostile after six months. The country actually is fatal to the Englishman in the minor key. For example, the Quakers, who are such an admirable foil to the assertive English type, became earthworms in India and got the housemaid's knee by cringing to Hindu Gurus—not the religious Gurus against whom they were protected by their own religion, but the political Gurus. This abject servility used to surprise me as much as the infatuation of the charming granddaughter of Queen Victoria for Rasputin.

If that could happen to the morally sound Quakers what could not happen to Forster? An Englishman who could take up employment under a petty Indian prince as his private secretary and Heaven knows what else—Heaven certainly knew and perhaps also the Agent to the Governor-General in Central India—such an Englishman was not likely to be better than a shrimp. In normal circumstances Forster would have gone native and become a character like Kipling's McIntosh Jellaludin, who left a long rigmarole of a book for which he made the claim that 'what Mirza Murad Ali Beg's book is to all other books on native life, will my work be to Mirza Murad Ali Beg's'. Strickland Sahib went through it and remarked that the man was either an extreme liar or a most wonderful person, and he thought the former.

But Forster was saved from going native by being inoculated with the venom of that brood of rattlesnakes—the Bloomsbury Group. They put everybody off their scent by masquerading as swaggering puppies when in reality they had the venom, fangs, and rattles of the snake. In the history of the decline and fall of Britain these arrogant triflers will be shown as the pipers who marched at the head of the procession which dragged the sacrificial beast to the altar.

The cheekiness imbibed from the Group enabled Forster to survive his life in India and resume his career as an author in England. But he nursed a grievance against the British official hierarchy because he was not treated with consideration by them, and like all weaklings he gave expression to his sense of grievance, not through anger, but through malice. He tried to square his account with the officials by slandering a great historical phenomenon. There is no man who is more despicable than the writer who uses his gifts to settle personal scores. I hope I have earned the right to say this by praising Kipling and not admiring Forster.

Judged purely as a novel, *A Passage to India* can be regarded as the radical antithesis to Ethel M. Dell's imperialistic novels. But the assertive defeatism of the inter-war years, which had as one of its elements a feeble anti-imperialism, gave this novel its status, and made Forster a sort of literary Earl of Shaftesbury. His reputation survives because the process of decomposition of British greatness is not yet complete. The British people still need consolation in the shape of a moral apology for the loss of their position. It is owing to this that a book which stinks in the nostrils is supposed to be giving off the odour of sanctity.

So, those who would write about India are left without guidance from the past, and consequently deprived of the base which only tradition supplies for a new advance. This disadvantage could be overcome by an authentic and clearly felt purpose behind the writing. But this is absent because the interest which alone could create it, is not felt.

After independence there was some curiosity about the sequel to the abandonment of the Empire, and also a good deal of unjustified expectation. Both have been snuffed out by the legatees of British rule. Today the only interest which seems to keep writing on India going is about Hindu religion and erotic art.

Now, Hindu spirituality was a snare for Occidentals even when their interest in it was scholarly and healthy. It is now only a mirage to lure a morally and spiritually degenerate West. When I read or hear the drivel about our philosophy here, I say: Yoga and Vedanta are for those Europeans who have accepted defeat; for the European who still wants to be victorious there are only two things: Beef and brandy. Osbert Sitwell had an intuitive perception of this when he said that all Englishmen of genius had gout. In their obsession with psychology Occidentals have forgotten physiology. The whole Western interest in Hindu spirituality is anti-biological. Witness for instance Aldous Huxley. What a fate was it for the scion of a dynasty of zoologists to have become only a subject of study for them by transforming himself into a jellyfish!

Besides, what the West takes for Hindu spirituality is not the real thing, in which there was no humbug. On the other hand, Hindu erotic art is not also what it is represented to be. What a scandal I would raise if I said, as I have reason to do, that the erotic sculpture for which we were once abused and are now extolled was most probably derived from portable examples of Greek and Roman erotic art which reached India.

For the most part, writing about India today is mere potboiling. I do not object to that. If three-quarters of living is potboiling, three-quarters of writing is bound to be the same. Even that great snob, Lord Chesterfield, conceded to potboilers the right to produce books and have their readers. He declared in a neat epigram: 'Let blockheads read what blockheads wrote.'

But potboiling becomes dangerous when the last quarter is not left for writers who have a sense of vocation. Long ago I was taught the distinction between a vocation and a trade by a Kashmiri shawl merchant. Finding him showing his goods in a friend's house I observed politely: 'I have heard that you deal in shawls.' 'No, Sahib,' he replied smiling, 'I only keep the belly going.' Some writers at least should show that spirit. British writers on India do not.

But you will ask why Indians are not filling the vacuum created by them. Up to a point they are trying. However, to my thinking their performance is not different from that of British authors. This really is the saddest part of the story, and the situation has been inexorably created by history. The introduction of the English language and literature brought about a mental revolution in India to which even the European renaissance does not furnish a parallel. There was also a competent knowledge of English. This could have led educated Indians to make an effort to contribute to English literature. In fact, both the creator of modern Bengali poetry and of modern Bengali fiction wrote their first works in English. But the enterprise was killed by the British themselves.

The poet was asked by an eminent English educationist to give up English and write in Bengali, while the novelist felt that English led nowhere and did the same. The advice of the educationist was realistic, for in those days no Indian would have got a publisher in England. What was perverse was the reaction of the British in India to our use of English in any way. They showered insults on us for this. This hostility created an emotional revulsion, and when Indians found deep and intimate satisfaction in creating a literature of their own and in reading it, they remained true to it.

Nonetheless, the entire inspiration together with the contents and forms of their writing came through the English language. As a result, a paradoxical literary situation was created, and it still continues. I can describe it only with the help of a scientific analogy. It is as if the substance of our literature was coming to us borne on Hertzian waves, and could be made audible only through the loudspeakers which our own languages were. Minds which were formed by the English language were forced to remain inarticulate in English. That is the greatest crime of the British people against their own culture.

However, after the First World War Indians began to emerge as authors. The external impulse behind that was the award of the Nobel Prize to Tagore. Other Indian writers thought they were no worse than he, and began to get their works translated into English. I have been told that the Swedish Academy is flooded with applications from India. One Indian poet not only announced in the newspapers that he was a candidate, but that he was also highly recommended. But, of course, it would be a reflection on the intelligence of Indian writers in general to think that they go beyond just daydreaming about the prize when they write in English.

The real encouragement from the success of Tagore came from the hope that the works of Indian authors might be accepted and recognized. However, those on whom this hope worked strongly formed special groups of Indians: first, those who had literary inclinations but could not write in any Indian language; next, expatriates; and finally those whose mother tongues had only a minor or no literature. All the notable Indian writers of English have come from these groups. That has given to their works a special character. They have written without the freedom to be natural, and so their writing has lacked inwardness and originality. Generally, it has been *ersatz*. Even for them it is a flower from a secondary bud.

But this artificial or secondhand quality has also a deeper cause. The Indian writers of English do not realize that authorship in that language is not a matter of linguistic competence alone. The whole personality must become Westernized without any loss of the capacity to respond to things Indian correctly. In short, what is needed is a Western *Weltanschauung* and even a Western neural sensitivity, which in its turn requires vitality. This is never sustained by the Indian manner of living. I provoke both anger and derision in India by saying that even the kind of English acceptable to Western publishers cannot be written by anyone living on the Indian diet. If that is half a joke, at least I act on it *in toto*. For thirty-five years I have not as a rule taken Indian food. That is the basic innovation I claim to have made as a writer in English.

In the general run of Indian writers in English the inadequacy of vitality produces two results. The sincere ones cannot bear the burden of Westernization and revert to their traditional mental heritage, to become Puran Bhagats. The worldly ones become potboilers like the British writers. The Indian contribution to the so-called Commonwealth literature comes from this group. But it is developing in such a way that you may eventually need a literary Race Relations Board to deal with complaints of colour prejudice. In the universities such complaints have already made their appearance.

I do not belong to their class, and they reject me equally. They say that I am not a creative writer like them. Recently, the Director of the Indian Centre of Commonwealth Literature even said that I write Bengali English, i.e. Babu English. I make no grievance of all that, because I have declared publicly that so far as I write in English I am not an Indian writer but only a writer in India. I need not write in English to satisfy literary ambition. I am an author in Bengali as well, and probably the only writer in India who uses English as well as his mother tongue for major expression. My literary standing was established as long ago as 1927 on the strength of my Bengali writings. I write in English for a different purpose.

That would exclude my writings from literature in a strict sense. They are the product of two urges. In my young days the Indian nationalist movement was very idealistic, and it taught us that beyond worldly aspirations we had a great duty, which was to re-establish the greatness of our country and civilization. I also developed very early in life a strong desire for knowledge as an aid to living. These two combined to make me think of becoming a writer. Later, when I found modern Indian culture perishing, I felt I had to fight for it. So, instead of being a literary man, I am really a preacher, as you also must be finding me to be. This made the employment of English by me inevitable, for a preacher wishes to have the largest possible audience.

But in spite of being a preacher by function I stand at the door of literature by virtue of my methods. I have realized from my reading of literature that no other means of communication has the same power to convert minds. So I go to literature in the first instance for subsidiary devices to reinforce even a political argument. For example, in 1946, only a year after Labour's sensational electoral victory I was trying to deflate the balloon of its pretensions and I said in an article that the Labour administration was going to close an era, and not open a new one. But I knew that Labour had different shades and described them with symbols taken from a favourite novel.

Sturdy English Labour, pledged to a socialistic programme [I wrote] was not more frightening than Thomas Hardy's Farmer Oak married to the widowed Bathsheba . . . But behind him stood Sergeant Troy, not dead as in the novel but very much alive, very much baleful, and very much bent on mischief . . . Our unfortunate country—India—might figure as Fanny of the piece, destined to be seduced and abandoned by the meretricious English Leftist, as fickle in his loves as in his coldnesses, and sloppily egoistic in everything.

This sort of trick I had learnt from the essay on association and dissociation of ideas by Remy de Gourmont, whom I had read in early life. But I should add that such devices are legitimate only when you have forgotten all about technique. I had.

I am more directly literary in another aspect of my writing, namely, in my preoccupation with the sounds and rhythms of English. This arises from my awareness that literature like music is an art which unfolds in time and cannot be seen as a whole in space, and that any art that does so cannot be grasped unless it has a rhythmic structure. Nobody taught that more assiduously than the Greek and Roman rhetors. Even the Christian theologians knew this and employed the established prosodic devices. Thus, the so-called Athanasian Creed, which makes a string of irrational statements, becomes irresistible owing to the music of its prose. Written according to both the quantitative and stress systems of late Latin, it made use of the effects of cretic spondee, trochee spondee, etc., of the old system, and of *cursus planus*, *cursus velox*, etc., of the new. Having learnt all this I became convinced that no prose could be effective unless it was written, as it were, musically.

In writing English this set me an almost insoluble problem. I was wholly ignorant of the sounds of English as uttered by its natural speakers. I had not learnt the language from Englishmen. In those days there was neither radio nor talking films. Actually, when I published my first book in London and New York at the age of fifty-four, I had not had six hours of conversation with Englishmen in my whole life, and I could not wholly follow their pronunciation. Therefore I was almost paralysed by the fear whether my English would sound like the English spoken by you.

To overcome this difficulty I adopted a method which worked in practice. I read the great examples of English prose, sounding them in my ears, and from that acquired some idea, perhaps a wrong one, of the sound effects. And I wrote my own English sounding it in the same way, and passed it if there was agreement in error.

If all this has made me a literary craftsman, it has also made me a freak, and my case is not relevant to the general situation of writing about India. Nevertheless, I shall not say like the Preacher: Of making of books there is no end. I shall say, *we need books*, for we Hindus believe that there is no salvation without knowledge.

However, as things stand, it is futile to expect even a search for true knowledge from fellow-Indians today. They are all either benumbed or bemused by chauvinism. Even now truth about India can be discovered only by a Western mind which is faithful to its own intellectual heritage. But the handicaps are serious, especially for British authors. I shall round off my say by considering the two major ones.

In the forefront there is one inherited difficulty, which has been aggravated by the severance of the practical connection. It springs from the so-called empiricism of the Englishman. Julien Benda's joke about it was that there was a dog which knew its master when standing but not when seated, and that dog was English. This has made Englishmen raise the bogey of India's infinite diversity, and put that forward as an excuse for lack of understanding. The bewilderment did not matter when observation and the response to it in action were directly linked. But when only interpretation is the issue it is a serious disadvantage.

The obsession with diversity reminds me of a mad man we had in Nicholson Park in Delhi. His mania was to pick up the leaves which fall in February and March, and count them one by one. One day he darted towards my wife, who was giving our golden retriever its walk, and asked: '*Ye kuttaka ketne bal?*—How many hairs has this dog got?' The Englishman was always asking about India: *Ye kuttaka ketne bal?* That was not the best way to know the animal, though it could help in picking off the ticks.

There is, however, an efficacious method, which is to apply what Pascal has called the spirit of geometry as opposed to the spirit of finesse. He himself defined it as follows: 'The principles are palpable but remote from common experience, so that people find it difficult to turn to them, being unused to doing so; but if they only would, the principles will be seen clearly; and one must have a total falsity of spirit to reason wrongly about principles which are so starkly plain that it is almost impossible to overlook them.' That applies to India, for the country, with all its diversity, has an underlying simplicity. On the other hand, the spirit of finesse which confines itself to details will always be baffled.

But in addition there is a far greater difficulty which arises from the present historical situation of the British people. I hope I shall not offend you if I call it decadence, for in historical thinking the word stands only for the old age of a nation. In it there may be decline of power and creativity but nothing discreditable.

This too engaged my mind after the end of the war. I loved England, and you know what strange fits of passion a lover can have, how he may be suddenly terrified by the thought that his Lucy might be dead. But I was also seeing things which I did not like. So I tried to reassure myself by writing, this too in 1946:

> The main task is to rescue English politics from a fussiness and sentimentality unbecoming of its maturity and endow it with a mellowness, serenity, and ease consistent with that maturity. There can be no question of any loss of strength or dignity in the pursuit of repose . . . But this repose in strength is unattainable unless knowledge and wisdom are added to intuitive impulses. There could be no greater pity in history than for a great nation to have its maturity wearing only the flippant simper of the demagogue or the drawn unloveliness of the doctrinaire. Every great nation expects its maturity to be crowned by a golden Augustanism. Perhaps it may still come, but the signs are not propitious.

After thirty years I find that it is my fears and not my hopes which have come true, and in a manner which even my fears could not anticipate. Yet the evils do not lie in the objective conditions. Marcus Aurelius said that even in a palace life can be lived well. Living in England for the last six years, I have discovered that so it can be even in the Welfare State. What is wrong is the psychological situation which has no necessary connection with the objective state of affairs. There is in it defeatism, passivity, and class hatred on an immense background of drabness, relieved only by sordidness, sensuality, indiscipline, and trifling. English writers polluted by this psychological environment cannot deal with India.

I do not say that because I think, being decadent, you are unqualified to write about a country which after gaining independence is trying to build up a new life like the Japanese in the Meiji era. I do not nurse such an illusion. The truth is that we in

India have left even decadence far behind and are now only fossils. A thin coating of fungus on them does not make any difference to the underlying petrifaction. Thus, for centuries the Indian people have been insensitive to sorrow or happiness. Even when under British rule there was relative ease in living for them, the British administrators wondered if in actual fact they felt that they were happy. Lord Lawrence as Viceroy gave his answer quoting Virgil. They ought to, he said, *sua si bona norint*—if they but knew their good fortune. They did not.

Yet a great sorrow gnawed at their heart at the deepest level of consciousness. Against that, they protected themselves with an apocalyptic faith without any eschatology. They have always reckoned on deliverance without even caring to inquire how, when, and in what form it would come. This has enabled them to endure any deprivation in the present.

When, however, this faith has not been adequate, they have fallen back on two things as their last resource. These are—*Tamasha* or gregarious fun, and hatred. To them their religion is *tamasha*, voting is *tamasha*, the deaths of Gandhi and Nehru were *tamasha*, even tyranny is *tamasha*. When this fails they burst out in hatred, and quench both the boredom and the festering ache underneath in blood. That is the broad pattern of Indian life as revealed by the spirit of geometry. The spirit of finesse will hear only the chatter about progress which mocks that existence.

A British writer of today, if he is capable of feeling, will display either anger, or partisanship, or flippancy without understanding what he is seeing. The unfeeling will turn out just grist to the mill. Perhaps some day an Englishman will be born who after participating in all the contemporary debauch, sedition, and levity, will turn his back on them and write a new *City of God* like St Augustine. He will also be capable of writing about India. Till then, I would rather the British people forgot all about India than be reminded of her existence by the kind of writing which is now current.

FORWARD TO NATURE

JOHN STEWART COLLIS, FRSL

Read 13 November 1975:
Vincent Cronin, FRSL, in the Chair

WHEN Byron once criticized Leigh Hunt's style, Hunt replied
that his style was 'a system'. 'When a man talks of system,' said
Byron to Moore, 'his case is hopeless.' I'm inclined to be equally
chary of the word 'experiment'. He who can does, he who can't
experiments, I sometimes feel. And I'm not terribly keen on the
word 'innovator'. Certainly I don't see myself in that light. With
me it has simply been a matter of acting on instinct and common
sense in accordance with the way my mind works. Many writers
are more or less the victims of the way in which their particular
talent makes them slant their pens.

Before going a step further let me tackle the supposed problem
of the scientist versus the poet: the scientific approach versus the
poetic approach. Is there a real difference here, a real gap: and if
so can it be bridged? In my opinion there is a great difference
between these two approaches. I don't regret this, and I don't see
any reason to 'reconcile' them any more than to reconcile two
entrance doors to a house, or two different games such as rugger
and soccer.

Take an example of the scientific approach to nature. Darwin
wrote a book called *The Formation of Vegetable Mould Through
the Action of Worms*. A great title for a great book on a great
subject. For the worm is great, though it might not seem so. Eye-
less, voiceless, earless, legless, armless, faceless, it looke merely like
a squirming piece of flesh. But by virtue of its strong muscles,

its two stomachs, and its false teeth, it can carry out remarkable works. William Blake spoke of the tiger in glowing terms. He also stooped down and gazed upon the worm. 'Image of weakness, art thou but a worm? I see thee as an Infant wrappèd in the lily's leaf.' In this he was perhaps being sentimental. For the worm is more powerful than the tiger. What with its plough-ing, its harrowing, its manuring, its draining, its airing, its level-ling, and even its creating of soil, it adds to the wealth of nations and governs the destiny of man; and, given time and condition, could remove a mountain and cause a city to vanish from the face of the earth.

Interesting facts. Not easy to establish. The scientist is the man who establishes facts. The poet is the man who sings them. Con-sider what the satisfactory establishment of a fact involves from a scientific point of view. Darwin wanted to make sure that worms are deaf. He went out into a field at Downe in Kent, and lying beside a worm, played a trombone at it. The worm did not turn. He then experimented in the same way with thirty other worms. They did not turn. Darwin was not yet satisfied. One of his sons went out to another field, and selecting fifty more worms played the bassoon at them. They did not turn. Darwin was still not satisfied. His second son went into a further field and blew a trumpet at twenty-two other worms. They did not turn. It was only then that Darwin concluded that it would not be inappro-priate to claim that worms are deaf.

Now if you or I wished to assure ourselves that worms have no ears, and went and played the trombone at ten or even five of them, and if they did not squirm we would probably not hesitate to proclaim that worms are hard of hearing.

We may laugh. And perhaps there is some slight element of comedy in the solemnity of such investigation. But I am entirely on the side of Darwin—(though I have exaggerated a little). In order to really establish facts it is essential to black the chimney in this way. Scientists cannot afford to generalize from a few par-ticulars. Anyone can propose a theory on the basis of trifling par-ticular instances. We have to suffer superficial pundits in every field, on gardening, on diet, on health, on mechanics, on clim-atology, on psychology, on occult matters right and left, when the most dubious rostrums are pronounced on the basis of trumpery evidence, and rash theories advanced on the most perfunctory of incidents. True scientists will have none of this: they concentrate with such patience and determination upon nature that they can actually comprehend the composition of matter. They get re-

markable results. They were able last month to take a close-up
photograph of the planet Venus!

These thorough-going investigators are not using the aesthetic
faculty, and are inclined to leave aesthetics alone. There are exceptions of course, but Darwin himself lamented the deteriora-
tion of his aesthetic faculty, declaring that he couldn't bear poetry
and that reading Shakespeare made him sick—or words to that effect.

The poet, on his part, is not drawn towards investigation. He
concentrates upon the finished article, the object. He looks at it
till he can really see it. He concentrates his imagination upon it—
that is the instrument he uses, not fancy or invention. Fancy is
the power to see what is not there: imagination is the power to see
what is there. Creative imagination, I would say, after an initial
inspiration, is for the rest sheer intellectual concentration until
the object is seen in its pristine essence, significance, mystery,
beauty, and glory. Wordsworth called it 'Reason in her most ex-
alted mood.' And if scientists regard poets with little interest, it is
true that poets tend to be blind to science.

As a boy I was not only blind to science but I detested it—so
strongly was my bent in the opposite direction. It was called
'stinks' at my school—and for me it stank. It was not until some
twenty-five years later that I became interested in science, and I
still have no scientific leaning. I don't want to make experiments.
I don't want to discover things. If I were to discover some pre-
historic skull in my garden I doubt if I would be unduly excited,
or have any feeling beyond Alas, poor Yorick. In any case things
never work out for me satisfactorily if I do undertake anything in
the way of a scientific inquiry. Perhaps I can give an example of
what I mean in a passage from *Down to Earth*. I was referring
again to Darwin's book on worms, and on how they could bury
objects, from stones to cities, if left alone long enough:

One day when strolling in a great Cathedral Cloister, I
observed that the grass in the middle contained many flat-
slabbed tombstones, some modern, some quite ancient. How
interesting, I thought, here I shall be able to see the results of
worm burial before my eyes. I observed a modern stone, 1921,
how it was level with the grass, and near it another stone, 1804,
which had sunk a considerable bit. This was excellent. I
walked round so that I might see the old tombstones well sunk
while the newer ones were still on the surface. I came to
Martha Hunt, of Beloved Memory, dated 1870, and then to
Nathaniel Groves, Resting in the Lord, dated 1791. But

Martha Hunt's tombstone had sunk lower than that of Nathaniel Groves! Trying not to notice this I passed on and continued to conduct my researches. Some of the stones conformed to the requirements of the theory, but not all. Coming to Arthur Mackensie, of Beloved Memory, dated 1801, and then upon Elizabeth Wakefield, in Loving Memory of, dated 1910, I was grieved to observe that the latter was lower than the former.

I need not say that I do not at all dispute Darwin's findings. Apart from the fact that many reasons could doubtless be given as to why these particular stones were as they were, I feel confident that no fault lay with the worms. It is merely psychologically impossible for things of this kind to work out well for me. Had Darwin experimented here we may be sure that the tombstones would have arranged themselves in the proper order. The poet is the man who sees. The philosopher is the man who thinks. The man-of-action is the man who knows what to do. The scientist is the man who discovers. These are special kinds of men as is soon found by any Tom, Dick, or Harry who, assuming the role of one, attempts to see or to think or to lead or to experiment. I fear I have nothing of the scientist in me, nothing of the naturalist or botanist; I shall never propose a theory supported by experimental proof, I shall never discover anything, never make new things known. I am content to make known things new.

But, you may say, I am regarded as an Ecologist—indeed on the back of the Penguin edition of my books there is the claim: 'He is the poet among modern ecologists.' Well, it is good to have a label; it argues that someone has read or may conceivably read one's books. But I am not an ecologist. True, I have written about ecology twenty or thirty years ago, but what I said was entirely derivative from the real dedicated ecologists who were writing at that time. I tried to bestow artistic shape upon their findings. I was careful to do so whenever ecology was relevant to my subject. Especially with regard to trees since the history of trees is aligned with the history of man. But I didn't use the word ecology till about the last page of my book, *The Triumph of the Tree*. I used the phrase—the Natural Order. I took pains to give shape to what is meant by the Natural Order, and to show how when it is abused we see the Revenges of Nature; in ancient times resulting in Lost Cities in the Jungle, Buried Cities in the Desert, terrible Chinese Floods and Rivers of Sorrow; and how in the nineteenth century in North America after the ruthless campaign against the Indians, the campaign against the prairies, the campaign against the animals, the campaign against the trees above all, there inevitably followed erosion and dust and 'the Grapes of Wrath'.

I have always been careful to do my stint on ecology whenever my theme demanded it. In my book *The Moving Waters* I devoted a special chapter to the Sins Against Water. In fact I open with these words—

> How can we sin against water, you may ask? We can sin against soil. We can sin against crops. We can sin against trees. But even as the sun shines upon the evil and upon the good, so the rain falls alike upon the just and the unjust, and as we cannot diminish the rays of the sun, neither can we lessen the abundance of the waters. That is true. Yet we can sin against water. We can defile it. A river may be used as a water supply. It may be used as a highway. It may be used as a means of power. But the time came when it was put to a further service—it was used as a *sewer*.

Indeed, I am strong on sin. Even in my book on Light I have a piece on the Sins Against Light . . . Oil is really squashed fish—the massed remains of marine organisms buried in sedimentation. And I made this observation:

> Stranger than the cliffs of Dover bricked by the shells of globigerina; stranger than coal which is sunshine fused with fossilized forest, is this further digging up of old sunshine consolidated by marine organisms in the depths of the sea, eventually to be found after the shifting of the waters under the plains and deserts of the earth. They went down, these little things, these plant creatures, they lay down in their massive millions to rest peacefully for evermore. They have risen from the dead—as oil. From oil they have changed into light and speed— and also, how well we know it!—into endless conflict of nations and the graves of men dying in the cause of commerce.

I wrote this in 1955. That last remark is still more pertinent today, for since our manner of life is based chiefly on squashed fish, a few haughty Eastern gentlemen on the far-flung deserts of Arabia can actually dictate to us what we shall do at Piccadilly Circus.

But the fact that I have attempted to bestow literary shape upon aspects of ecology does not entitle me to be called an ecologist any more than to be called a physicist because I threw into relief the meaning of the new alchemy.

I'm sorry about these negatives, but they are rapidly leading me to my positive. First I would like to bring into historic perspective the changing relation between Science and the Arts. I won't go back very far—just to December 28th, 1817, when Lamb, Keats, Wordsworth, and Benjamin Haydon dined together. They discussed the merits of Homer, Shakespeare, Milton, and Virgil; and as the evening advanced, Lamb becoming slightly the better for drink, began to abuse Haydon for putting Newton's head into a picture he had just finished, 'a fellow', he declared, 'who believed nothing unless it was as clear as three sides of a triangle'. Then Lamb and Keats agreed that Newton had destroyed all the poetry of the rainbow by reducing it to its prismatic colours. They all ended with a toast 'drinking Newton's health and confusion to mathematics'.

A trivial incident perhaps, but indicative of a new mood, a feeling that science was becoming an enemy of the arts. This was a new idea, for from the Middle Ages to the eighteenth century the 'sciences' were regarded as 'the arts of the mind'. Every branch of learning was regarded as a *scientia*, and whether the subject was grammar, geometry, logic, music, art, the term 'sciences' or 'arts' could be used. You went to the university to study the sciences, that is to learn things—a university was a unifier of knowledge. The term Philosophy was still widely used to define Science as we now understand it, while a 'philosophical apparatus' meant a scientific apparatus; and when in the sixteenth century Sir Philip Sidney spoke of a tale which holdeth children from play and old men from the chimney corner, it was not of stories he was thinking, but of knowledge.

It is difficult to understand why Newton should have caused such a change in the attitude of the poets—of some poets, I should say. Especially Keats. Science, he declared, 'will clip an Angel's wings, conquer all mysteries of rule and line . . . unweave a rainbow.' It is hard to understand why Keats, with his powerful mind, and passionately held belief in what he called the Principle of Beauty in All Things, should have been upset by prismatic colours or 'secondary qualities', since there is no reason why the chalice of the yellow tulip should seem less pure a cup because its colour does not strictly belong to it, but was eight minutes ago in the sun. That fact is not a minus but a plus—it is just a further miracle.

Newton did not affect all the literary men in this way. Both

Pope and Swift used science as good material for their art in terms of commentary or satire. Thus Pope:

> Go, wondrous creature! Mount where Science guides.
> Go, measure earth, weigh air, and state the tides.
> Instruct the planets in what orbs to run,
> Correct old Time, and regulate the sun;
> Go, teach Eternal wisdom how to rule—
> Then drop into thyself, and be a fool.

It is good to be reminded how fine an instrument the heroic couplet is for swift assessment and pungent comment. In many ways Pope is quite up to date in spite of his odious axiom that the proper study of mankind is man.

John Donne made the famous observation—

> And new Philosophy calls all in doubt.
> The Element of Fire is quite put out;
> The Sun is lost, and th' earth and no man's wit
> Can well direct him where to look for it.

Those words are often quoted as being written by a man who felt keenly that the new learning had thrown men into confusion. I don't think he minded much; quite likely he enjoyed the opportunity that Science gave him to be clever and allow epigram to enrich his rhyme. The man who really did mind was Blake, who declared war upon Newton for twenty years. Blake was easily upset. He was so inspired, so 'God-intoxicated' a man that scientists could really anger him. 'Do you think I simply see a little round disc about the size of a shilling?' he asked while regarding a sunset. 'Oh no, I see a company of the Heavenly Host crying holy, holy, holy Lord God Almighty!' He shouted manifestoes against Science. He took a knife and cut people's heads up. He made a tremendous slash through the skull neatly dividing the cranium into two equal parts. In one half he discovered vision, imagination, intuition; in the other half he discovered reason, analysis, and experiment: one was spiritual, the other materialistic; one right, the other wrong, one good, the other bad. The way of analysis, he declared, was the way of corruption and mockery, the words 'reason' and 'experiment' were the slogans of the devil, and this was the way of Descartes and of Locke, and these were the slogans of Bacon and Newton.

> Mock on, mock on Voltaire, Rousseau;
> Mock on, mock on, 'tis all in vain!
> You throw the sand against the wind,
> And the wind throws it back again.

And every sand becomes a Gem
Reflected in the beams divine;
Blown back they blind the mocking Eye
But still in Israel's paths they shine.

The Atoms of Democritus
And Newton's particles of Light
Are sands upon the Red Sea Shore
Where Israel's tents do shine so bright.

Great stuff—though I do not know what it means. What is clear
however is that Blake was very angry with the theory of Secondary Qualities. As I say, he was easily upset. He even got a severe
stomach complaint at the thought of Wordsworth's pantheism.

Wordsworth's case is rather peculiar. In this context he is
generally identified as having said that it was 'murder to dissect',
and that the scientist was the sort of chap who would 'peep and
botanize upon his mother's grave'. Well, anyone might say
something like that when confronted with a certain type of
person. What is not so well recognized is that in his important
Preface to the *Lyrical Ballads* Wordsworth declared that he looked
to the time when 'the remotest discoveries of the Chemist, the
Botanist, or Mineralogist will be as proper objects of the Poet's
art as any upon which it can be employed. If the time should ever
come when what is now called Science, thus familiarized to men
shall be ready to put on, as it were, a form of flesh and blood, the
Poet will lend his divine spirit to aid the transfiguration.' In quoting that passage in my book called *Paths of Light* twenty years
ago, I added: 'Those words might well be used to-day as the
apologia or manifesto of those who believe that the time has come
for the poet to exhibit before the public gaze the spoils and tro-
phies of the investigators.'

A few years ago I listened to a broadcast programme lasting for
about ten minutes each day for a week, when the subjects of
Water and of Fire and of Air and other Elements were tackled.
We heard first a scientist saying what Water is, its combination of
hydrogen and oxygen and so forth, delivered in flat terms; and
then a poet, Ted Hughes, gave his version in a tremendously
poetical way. Those who like facts presented in scientificese will
have enjoyed the first man, while those who enjoy Ted Hughes's
poetry will have enjoyed his rendering of Water and Fire, etc.
Personally I was discouraged and cast down. Not by the speakers,
but by the assumption that there must be a great gap between
talking scientifically and talking poetically. I was obliged to tigh-

ten my belt to take in the scientist's information, and then tighten it some more to prime myself to face Mr Hughes's totally poetic assault. I wondered why it was assumed that one man alone could not have taken both parts instead of this ludicrous division and casting. At the beginning of this lecture I emphatically suggested that the scientific approach to reality and the poetic approach are quite different; but there is no reason at all why the findings of the scientists may not serve as material for the muse—and be, in fact, the very stuff of poetry.

I happen to believe that almost anything is subject to a clear statement in true literary form. The masters who persuaded me that this is possible were Macaulay, Cobbett, and Shaw. I further believe that if inspiration prevails the statement may be raised into the realm of poetry. The masters who persuaded me that this is possible were Ruskin and Herman Melville.

I find that when I have laid hold of the facts, when I have managed to work out from the often difficult terminology, exactly what has been said, what the thing amounts to, the result is generally surprising or paradoxical; the ordinary turns out to be often more extraordinary than the extraordinary, the material rather more immaterial than the immaterial, the natural rather more supernatural than the supernatural, and the invisible rather more concrete than the concrete.

Sometimes, having put the surprising facts squarely before the reader, I am at liberty to summarize them with a degree of accurate audacity (assuming that context and inspiration are favourable). Coal, we know, is squashed trees caused by sinking forests. Apparently at Essen in Germany, as many as one hundred and forty-five forests, each a land-surface on its own, after drinking the sunshine were lowered down, one on top of the other, and in course of time squashed into pulp and hardened into rock—rocks of carbon. We call it coal. In three million years the South Wales coalfield could be produced. I summarized in this way:

We take a piece of it in our hands, a black stone. It is carbon, it is sunshine shaped into a solid. It is a piece of the sun itself we hold, the blazing ball itself turned into the dirty darkness of this rock. It may be very cold, freezing to the touch on a winter's day; yet still it is the ancient furnace that we finger, it is heat made cold, a frozen burning beam. We do not doubt this for a moment. We know how to change it back, how make it into fire again. We put a piece of its own element in touch with it—its own essence, flame—and in a few minutes the box flies open and the trebly millioned years imprisoned sun streams out, and the ransomed rays that fell upon the ferns fall on us today.

That piece came near the beginning of my book on trees: near the end of it I mentioned how excited people were at the dawn of coal-mining—which of course is another branch of agriculture and forestry, though we dig deeper, cut without planting, and reap where we have not sown. 'We are living in an age,' declared George Stephenson, 'when the pent-up rays of that sun which shone upon the Carboniferous Forests of past ages, are being liberated to set in motion our mills and factories.' And I added:

We must allow a certain epic grandeur in their theme. The power was divined. The potential wealth was realized. The possibilities seemed boundless. Naturally there was a coal rush. Claims were staked out by the enterprising and adventurous, and messengers were sent down into the primitive forests. A strange journey indeed! Strange wanderings in those sunken lands! Pioneering down into the darkness, the travellers explored that green old world of long ago. They made perpendicular roads and descended as far as three miles into the buried woods. They carved out galleries within them. They ran trucks through tunnels chiselled from the petrified leavings of the rotten reeds. And as they passed along those corridors encased by the corrupted ferns, and penetrated ever further into the lost regions of the sunlit lands, the danger from gases obliged them to go in darkness with nothing to lighten their way save the phosphorescent gleam from dried fish. Eventually the Davy Lamp was invented; but until then they had to rely upon phosphorescent fish. A haddock, for instance, can be so luminous that it could be photographed by its own light. Burning without fire these lamps will not call forth force. It is a strange thought. It conjures up mystery upon mystery. In a coal mine there are forces that will leap forward in answer to a flame. Silence; stillness; the blackness of dawnless day; nothing living, nothing moving—such is a corridor in a mine. No life is there; but Force is sleeping there: animation is suspended in those inky halls. The entrapped sunshine is there—imprisoned for three million years of speechless night. A little flame will be enough to voice its presence. Strike a match—and suddenly that crunched and crouching power will leap out like a wild beast and rend the cage. So the early visitors to these lost forests of yesteryear were careful not to come with fire that would call forth the spirit of the ancient sun. The ineffectual flame they brought was cold and tame—a fireless torch upon a lifeless fish.

What I like to do, what I aim at if possible, is to conceal from the reader that I am making or about to make, a poetic assault. This may make you smile, since the preceding extracts hardly bear this out. But I did try. I thought that if I suddenly lowered my flight and referred to dry fish and the humble haddock, and talked about the Davy lamp, my literary arabesque wouldn't be too apparent. But back in the corridors of the mine and with the gases, poetry would keep breaking in. All the same, my method if I can call it such, is to embody the poetic element in such a way that I can spring a surprise on the reader, giving him a lift unawares. Thus with frost, for instance; having explained what frost is, how the molecules in icy atmosphere so closely combine as to become visible if given a base, I proceed:

> Yet not until we come close can we take in the full wonder of the work. All things are transfigured, even barbed wire and iron railings. Nor does it matter how tender or intricate or small the object is; without smudging, and without weighing down or breaking, the white print is cast. The spider's web hangs on the gate. Yesterday we might not have noticed it. Today it has caught and fixed the freezing vapour in its net—like a photograph developed from the negative. We behold a double miracle: the weaving of the web by the living crawling creature, and the weaving of the filaments of frost by the molecules that in another mode tread another loom.

I was careful to hide from the reader my intention to be poetical, for that might create a barrier between us; I kept the thing down with barbed wire and iron railings. If the style is raised unexpectedly while dove-tailed with sober statement, then the reader, taken by surprise and not by storm, can shift his vision without effort from the particular to the whole, from the area of fact into the realm of truth—sometimes called beauty.

I find myself working on the assumption that if I weigh the text down with some hard facts it is easier to rise—as if by some inverse law of gravitation. While writing about ploughing, I carefully went into the practical details of the job, the business of the coulter, the share, and the turn-furrow, and the operations involved—it is so much easier to do a thing than write about it. After which I could make a smooth rise upwards in a quiet manner.

The eye is severely engaged indeed, and yet there is opportunity, and a great inclination, to glance round at the scene as a whole—at the furrow-following seagulls, at the cloud galleons, at the sunset as the day closes. I could look down from a certain high field in Dorset towards a deep vale which was often filled with sunlight while I was in shadow. One afternoon the clouds so gathered that a shaft of sunshine was focussed upon one single field down there, as if the finger of God were pointing to a page which I must con for truth. I could not do so, being otherwise engaged, but was glad to see the text was there; and glad also many a time, to glance up as the chill winter day closed down, and see the elm-tree tracery write its hieroglyphics on the lofty scroll.

A few years ago the poet George Barker gave a broadcast, printed in the *Listener*, about prose poetry. What was this animal? he asked. It was inadmissible. It should not exist. It was a literary Loch Ness Monster. It was a Jubjub Bird. It was a Hippogryph. It was a Siberian Mastodon. It was a car with two wheels instead of four. It should not exist and therefore it did not exist. I formed the impression that Mr Barber was not terribly keen on prose poetry. Perhaps he had an axe to grind. Still, he had a point. If prose enters the province of poetry it cannot strictly be called prose. But it need not be called a monster.

I suppose that during the last fifty years more bad 'poetry' has been published than ever before, since people have been encouraged to cherish the illusion that because they have poetical feelings they are poets. This created a considerable mist through which the public had to peer to discern the true poets of the day, the few and the great. Those bad writers did not write in blank verse but in blank prose in the guise of free verse, for they dared not write in prose lest the feebleness of their substance and the hollowness of their pretentions be too nakedly exposed. They wrote inharmoniously and discordantly on the plea that this was the proper thing to do in a discordant age. They might just as well have said, as Dr Johnson did in another context, that 'he who drives fat oxen should himself be fat'. But as anyone can write badly on the ground that it is a bad world, it seems hardly worth while; and since the purpose of art is to bestow order upon chaos and to illuminate the darkness, it is a pity that so much publicity should have been given to these people bearing false witness against beauty and adhering to the principle of ugliness in all things. For amidst such a deluge of misappliance and misapprehension it is difficult to say the simplest thing about poetry without someone uttering some such phrase as 'It's a matter of opinion'—an assertion as inadmissible in aesthetics as it is in morals or in law.

There is such a thing as pure poetry. There is such a thing as pure prose. There is such a thing as pure verse. Take an example of the last—from Rudyard Kipling's *The Sleepy Sentinel*.

> Faithless the watch that I kept, now I have none to keep.
> I was slain because I slept—now I am slain I sleep.
> Let no man reproach me again for whatever watch is unkept.
> I sleep because I was slain; they slew me because I slept.

Strong words. Cast in so taut a form that the sense swiftly penetrates to the mind and pierces to the heart. It has nothing to do with prose. Nor is it poetry. (Though, of course, not seldom Kipling did write poetry.) It seems to me that generally speaking poets use a form of verse in which they can at intervals embody moments of poetry. Moments of true poetry are inevitably rare. They can occur in the middle of a poem, or as often happens, the first stanza is the real thing—pillared by good verse or bad verse. May I take a single example—of poetry embodied in the middle of verse.

> Thin, thin the pleasant human noises grow;
>   And faint the city gleams;
> Rare the lone pastoral huts: marvel not thou!
> The solemn peaks but to the stars are known,
> But to the stars, and the cold lunar beams:
> Alone the sun arises, and alone
>   Spring the great streams.

I would be surprised if all of us in this house did not respond to the magic of that poetic appeal. I would also be surprised if everyone can immediately recall the name of the poet, or if his name, the title of the poem. It is Matthew Arnold's *In Utrumque Paratus*. The lines which I have quoted are preceded by two stanzas of not memorable verse, and followed by three stanzas equally unmemorable. But how glad we are to have them!—for otherwise we would never have had the heaven-assaulting lines I have quoted. Perhaps the most obvious example of what I mean is Wordsworth's *Prelude*. We are happy that it is often extremely flat, since from that basis it can the better rise to great heights. And if poetry can be embodied in verse I don't see why it should not be embodied in prose.

It is not possible for me to determine just where I stand in this matter. A short time ago I came upon Flaubert's remark concerning 'the style that someone will invent some day, ten years or ten centuries from now. A style rhythmic as verse, precise as the language of science.' I was very struck by that. Had I been attempting something of the kind? The word 'invent' may seem a little odd, though; for the style would have to arise out of the particular man's bent of mind, his quick or slow grasp, his habit of reading, his nerves and digestion, his weaknesses, follies, and sins. It could not be passed on as you can pass an invention from one person having it to another person not having it. As for rhythm, I have long held the view that prose should scan even more imperatively than verse, especially when raised into the field of the imagination, otherwise the reader having been given a lift will be let down. (Of course anything in the way of a regular beat is fatal, and can easily be avoided.) The mention of *precision* much appealed to me. '. . . just the sky above him, the heaving dunes around, the cries of the circling sea-birds, and each wind-ruined wave renewed in endless riot . . .' I would claim that those words which I quote out of context from a book of mine on Columbus are very precise—Each wind-ruined wave renewed in endless riot—and that the precision demands no sacrifice whatever in terms of rhythm or vowel assonance. I would claim—for I am here to do myself a favour—the same thing for my dealings with speleology, and other ologies, and especially with what might seem a hard nut, the action of photosynthesis when the green cell in conjunction with sunlight creates the bricks which are laid to the foundation of the living world. I quote a few words from the summary:

In summary, the plants whose unbloodied kingdom stretches across the whole world, alone of all living things flourish without hunting and feed without slaughter, simply turning the sky into the tissues of their temples. The sheep consumes grass, the man consumes mutton . . . [I then say briefly what exactly the green cell does in combination with light, after which I was free to conclude with these words]—Thus the Circle, thus the Wheel turns for ever at its task; the vegetables perpetually decompose the carbonic acid, fixing the carbon and setting free the oxygen, while the animals take the food in the form prepared and perpetually breathe out that gas: the plants feasting upon the fumes of putrefaction and turning the relics of death into meadows of life, give us green pastures; so that even in our age, riddled as it is with scientific terminology, we can still pay tribute to the simplicity and grandeur of the theme with the rooted ancient words—*All flesh is grass.*

I lost you then—didn't I?—while I was on about the carbonic acid and the oxygen. No? Well, if not, I'm delighted. For I must have these things. I must have my acids and gases and dioxides—for only then can I give authority to my 'plants feasting upon the fumes of putrefaction . . .'

And by the way, since all flesh really *is* grass, I often feel inclined to answer people who ask me if I am a vegetarian—Yes, but I take my veg in the form of meat.

I did not find my way into this literary form, whatever label we may choose to attach to it, without fumbling about for some twenty years. In my twenties I wrote a number of short pieces in prose. Friends suggested to me that the stuff should be presented in free verse. So I put them into that form. Having done so it looked rather arbitrary and pointless, so I put them back into prose. Then they said—put them into a tighter form of blank verse. So I did that. But again it seemed pointless and I shoved them back into prose again. Then they said—make them rhyme. And I did that—but then shoved them back into prose. Then they said—*compose* them straight away in rhyme or free verse. And I did that. I composed quite a lot of pieces, generally in a great state of excitement and rapture—especially one day when coming upon Cleopatra's Needle on the Embankment, and reading from its base the account of how it was brought there, I sat down on the bench opposite and wrote a poem on it there and then. Eventually I had written enough pieces to make a volume. A few of them are not too bad: or perhaps, in Dr Johnson's phrase, were 'bad enough to please'. However, I had the sense to put them aside as pious relics of youthful endeavour.

I say that it took me some twenty years to find—not myself, for I have given up that search, but what I could do on paper. My chance came when I did something off paper. I became for six years an agricultural labourer—*not* a farmer worrying about his costs, but a worker without responsibility.

My ignorance about most things has always been excessive. This job gave me the stimulus to face my ignorance squarely; in fact to start from square one regarding any given thing. I found that if I did this I could give life to the subject, for the facts always turned out to be rather strange, and all I had to do was to state them. Take a single example. The potato has not entered literature very easily, and though Cobbett abused it and Byron rhymed it with Plato, it has made small appeal to the muse. When I gave my attention to it I came in for a surprise. After making my confession of ignorance as to how seed-potatoes create new potatoes, and having investigated through a season just what happened, and written down what I had observed, I then found that other people had been quite as ignorant about this as myself! When my piece was first published (in a periodical) it caused a stir. A headmaster lectured his school on the importance of the potato. A bishop preached a sermon on it. A Cabinet Minister declared that I had saved the potato—(I don't know what he meant). I stood in danger of being famous simply as a man who had looked a potato in the face. I am grateful to the spud but hope to hear no more about it. However, I then hastened to raise a fair number of other things, of other natural phenomena, from the basis of fact into the realm of truth, the area of mystery and beauty.

I did this by virtue of retaining the child's sense of ignorance, and attaining the adult's sense of wonder.

I often hear people say that so-and-so has 'retained the child's sense of wonder'. But that is hardly possible, since the child has no sense of wonder. It cannot have it. When the child is not taking everything for granted, it can display a bit of curiosity, a bit of invention, a bit of fancy that can grow eventually into Imagination which can scarcely be attained much before the age of twenty, if ever attained at all. For imagination is not only a question of inspiration but of sustained intellectual concentration. This is completely beyond the child. As children we are much more physically alive than later on; but we are mentally only half-alive—we are almost blind, we are almost deaf. Of course when we grow up we lose things: but what we lose are *thrills*, not wonder: riding a bicycle, flying a kite, finding chestnuts, a teenage love-letter, the taste of ice-cream—the list is endless. We lose all this, we can never recapture it. But as for Imagination, you might just as well expect children to be capable of Religion, to have a mystical experience which seldom happens, if ever, before the age of thirty-five. All they can have in the way of religion is a bit of theology or piousness.

In claiming that I retained my child-like ignorance and stupidity as my greatest assets, I am also bound to admit an increasingly developed adult's sense of wonder. If we do make this combination we reach the position of actually knowing what we don't know. I frequently meet people who don't know what they don't know, what they don't believe, what they don't understand, what they don't feel—this last so often leading to unseemly scenes of self-deception in personal affairs. It came as quite a shock to me to realize that I didn't really know that I didn't know that coal is squashed trees, that chalk is squashed shells, that oil is squashed fish: that I didn't know what the moon is. Really know, I mean, not the school way of knowing things. I didn't know what the moon is till I was fifty-six. At least I didn't know why it shone, because I didn't know that there is no such thing as sunshine *per se*. If there were such a thing then of course at night-time the sky above us would be blazing with light, but it is in darkness because the rays are totally invisible until they hit something, when a barren, lightless rock becomes a lamp—which we call the moon. When I have put the matter in this way to learned friends they have been kind enough to say that I have shown them the moon in a new light. I mention this in case you think my claim to ignorance as an asset is an idle boast.

I am willing to be read for my information alone. Especially by the young, if I can get past the barrier raised by the teaching profession, who regard me as their natural enemy. I wish to connect knowledge (since in Nature all things are all things) while they wish to separate it into compartments for the sake of schedule—imagine separating physics from botany, I ask you! So they regard me as their enemy—as I them. But I have not allowed this to daunt me too much. There is a great saying with regard to meeting enemies, and I recommend it to you: '*Meet them undaunted, and they will have no power to daunt thee.*'

I am willing to be read for my information alone, but that has not been my main purpose for writing. I am not interested in knowledge for its own sake. I like it to be for the sake of imagination. People sometimes come up to me and say—'Oh Mr Collis, I've just been reading a wonderful book which I'm sure you would enjoy; its all about trees, or worms, or ants, or dunghills, or chalk, or pot-holes'—some subject I have written about. And I have to reply—'I'm terribly sorry but I'm no longer interested in trees or worms or potatoes or what not, for I have already used them to play my tune, I have already used them for the purposes of my art.' And the person goes sadly away. But I mean it. The fact is I'm an art for art's sake man. As if I were almost a *fin de siècle* character. For when art is truly for art's sake it saves the world. When art is for art's sake it is for life's sake. To start with it is for the sake of beauty. And the case for being concerned with beauty is a very strong one, and it is this: that if we are not concerned with beauty, if we do not mind about it, then neither will we be concerned with ugliness nor mind about it; when people cease to be aware of beauty they cease to be aware of ugliness; when they cease to worship beauty they seem positively to worship ugliness— we look round and see that now truly has Mammon's kingdom come! For the awful thing is this: that while beauty can inspire us, ugliness can *frighten* us. For, to quote Martyn Skinner in one of his great poems—

> For ugliness, when it is harsh, extreme,
> Has power to terrify, and through the sense
> Work like a visionary experience.

I'll say it does!

When art is really for art's sake it is for the sake of that little lamp of imagination which illuminates the night, and with its loving kindness shields us from the dark sorrows of our weakness and sin. It is for the sake of philosophy, it is for the sake of religion. For what is it that the artist does? The poet, the painter, the musician, the sculptor, the architect, the dramatist, the novelist, the biographer, the historian, the singer, the actor, the dancer—when they are great artists what is it that they do? They come before us asserting nothing, arguing nothing, explaining nothing, pleading nothing, preaching nothing, questioning nothing—no! not asking what is the purpose of life, or the meaning of existence, or whether life is worth living, or whether there is a life to come, or whether there is a God or gods off stage, no, none of that! They hold up *a fragment of existence* before us, and we forget the questionings in our sense of the transcendent adventure of existence, a sense akin to exultation and gratitude for being alive. And so long as art exerts its spell upon us, we see that though life is a fearful catastrophe it is also a fearful joy; we don't seek salvation, for we feel that this recognition *is* salvation; we don't need to solve the problems, for they are dissolved in the experience; and we come upon the thought at last that the only answer to the riddle of the world is to be able to see the world.

WRITING FOR CHILDREN: SOME WASPS IN THE MARMALADE

JANE GARDAM, FRSL

Read 21 April 1977:
Vincent Cronin, FRSL, in the Chair

I AM rather ill at ease about this lecture because in it I am meant
to be discussing, as part of a series, how I have tried to break new
ground or apply new techniques in my chosen field, the children's book: and the truth is that I have not done anything of the
sort. When I sat down and considered how to explain what it is I
have been trying to do, it became harder and harder to say. Each
book I have written I have desperately wanted to write. Whether
or not they had anything to do with children never occurred to
me. I have never liked children's books very much. I don't read
very many. And I am frightened to death of declared children's
writers who can paraphrase the Plowden Report and know exactly what they are up to and where they are going.

I have not the faintest idea where I am going, whom I am
writing for or why I am compelled to write fiction at all. I cannot
tell you the relief it was to read of an interview with Iris Murdoch the other day where she said that she did not know either or
even whether she would continue to write at all. Novelists she
said 'are in the hands of the gods'. I was even more relieved when
I read the famous anecdote about Virginia Woolf discovered by
another woman in the lavatory of the London Library. 'Oh,' cried
the woman, 'I wonder if you are Virginia Woolf?' 'That,' said
Virginia Woolf, 'is what I often wonder.'

Once upon a time I did try to write a children's book—a book children would really love. I wrote it in the early 'sixties in the Public Library at Wimbledon after dropping my eldest children at their nursery school. I wrote painlessly for two hours a day with a smile upon my face. There are two kinds of people convinced that it is easy to write for children: mothers of five- to seven-year-old children and established authors of so-called adult fiction who need money fast and think it's a push-over. Both are mistaken.

I was mistaken. My book was called *The Astonishing Vicarage* and I wrote away among all the other Wimbledon mothers writing books with roughly the same name, the tramps clearing their throats over the *Times Literary Supplement* and old ladies burrowing in paper bags. When I had finished—it was a book about boarding-school children, tunnels, butterfly collections and clergymen—I sent it confidently off to a distinguished publishing house where I had a friend and expected to hear from her immediately.

But time passed, and grew heavy and it was several weeks before an embarrassed voice on the telephone said could she talk to me about it. About what? *The Astonishing Vicarage.* Talk now, said I. Long pause. 'Well, it's difficult.' 'You don't like it?' 'It's not that exactly,' she said, 'but I wonder if you realize that the curate is a homosexual?'

No, I said. No. Not really. I hadn't. Or if I had, maybe I had thought it hadn't mattered. Leonardo da Vinci—I said. I was really very disturbed. 'But he's not Leonardo da Vinci,' she said, 'he's a curate. Anyway children don't want to know—It's not what matters——' I agreed with this. 'The book is funny,' she said, 'but it is very strange.'

So I burnt it up, thank goodness, for it was quite hideously bad, not analysing at that moment the line, if there is one, between the novel and the tale for the young which has always anyway been a very wavering one. I did not even dwell on the interest to children of curates below the waist. I felt that such things were beyond me. As reviews of distinguished children's books began to take my eye—the 'sixties were certainly the time, says Maurice Sendak, when England and America were leading the world in children's literature, in narrative and lovely illustration—I began to see that I was a woman with too simple a mind to compete. Perhaps I thought I had better try something easy and where the critics were less clever and sometimes kind, a bit more widely educated: like the experimental novel, or the post-modernist novel. I rather liked the thought of the post-modernist breakthrough: the kind of novel now called sur-fiction or meta-fiction. I write so slowly when I am not in the Wimbledon Public Library—where there is every reason for writing fast—that by the time I had finished such a book it might not be as advanced as all that. It might even have become dated and make some money—rampant with homosexual curates in whom the children of the 'eighties could take innocent delight.

I would cut out the tunnels though; and the butterflies. In fact I would cut out a lot of things. There is a comforting school of thought—or development, or prediction—in modern fiction which advocates that more and more should be cut out, refined, reduced, released into anarchy and even form itself eventually abandoned. 'Forms are expendable,' says Ronald Sukenick, the American post-modernist—quite rightly. 'The novelist accommodates the ongoing flow of experience, smashing everything that impedes his sense of it, even if it happens to be the novel itself.' I liked this idea, daunting but brave. It has its dangers of course. Messing about with form you may be led inevitably, as John Fowles says in *Notes on an Unfinished Novel*, 'into a comic novel'. One must watch that. Though I'm glad P. G. Wodehouse and Jane Austen didn't. No—I was attracted by the destructive search, the seeking a thing until it ceased to exist. It might cure me of my obsession to write fiction altogether. Discover that the snark is really a boojum and you will be removed from the fight,

> you will softly and silently vanish away
> And never be met with again.

What a relief.

As I had spent so long before I had had my children doing post-graduate work on the eighteenth century and its classicism, it might be a lovely rest to consider formlessness. A void. Like Book One of *Paradise Lost*. I was never modest.

Well of course I did nothing of the sort. If writing a book for children was beyond me, considering a void was harder still. I returned not to the eighteenth century but to an almost bookless life, shepherd's pie by day and sewing name-tapes by night and only the old comforters to read to the children of an evening like Biggles and Tin-Tin and Beatrix Potter and Laura Ingalls Wilder and Richmal Crompton's *William*. It was a harrowing time, ending after some years when it occurred to me to write a book which sprang from a single image: of a child very young, under five, alone on a long beach, and to try to recreate the mystery of this time, the temporary freedom from fear and anxiety and the need for people which occurs now and then in very early childhood. John Fowles says that 'characters (in fiction) are like children who need constant caressing, concern, listening to, watching, admiring'. I don't agree with this entirely. Both characters in fiction and children I feel often need to be left to grow alone. Children ought not to be in need of consolation all the time, of fantasy, of myth, of being stroked like queen bees. In fact I think it's bad for them. Enid Blyton, a prime example of this consolation, is a long way from the truth though she's a lovely read for a lazy day when you're about seven. For children are usually very strong. William Golding's *Lord of the Flies* for example, once thought almost too painful to bear by the critics of the Sunday newspapers, was later set at advanced level in the schools and is now I understand an O level set book for fifteen-year-olds. Children were found able to take the murder by his companions of the spectacled boy better than we can. (Of course, according to John Wain, Golding is hardly a novelist at all—he is an allegorist of a kind I think which children instinctively understand.) But children have also almost appropriated—certainly they are fascinated by—the non-fictional novels of Orwell. I have seen a child weep and rage at *Animal Farm*. And in *Nineteen Eighty-Four* they can even take the rats.

So I tried to describe childhood in very bare words and clear colours and whether I thought I was writing poetry or painting I don't know. The exercise was impossible—trying to recreate moments of absolute peace that one is lucky if one remembers at all as soon as one is out of the pram—only I think sometimes afterwards on the edge of dream. I didn't bring the experiment off at all but I liked trying. It felt like real work and when the book was published as a children's book the critics said that I had entered the field of children's literature. When I wrote a novel about an older child and found that I was now called a children's writer I was very pleased indeed. The field was interesting and I certainly didn't make for the gate. Once—last year—I stepped outside to write a book about Jamaica which would not interest any child unless it was very peculiar—it wouldn't, as Robert Louis Stevenson said in 1881 (yes), 'fetch the kids'—but even though—perhaps because the critics said that they were pleased that I had moved to something serious, I found myself back in the field again writing another book about a child. This one I am delighted to say was published complete with a schoolmaster who gave bunches of flowers to little boys and a headmaster's wife who ran off with the captain of the school. Nobody turned a hair, least of all the children who are used to all that, being near to it.

But nobody fancies the idea of 'being cut in two like a wasp in the marmalade' and I do see that there are tiresome dangers in being thought to write for children only, unless you are very good indeed. A genius like Carroll. Some of the best new writers do state ferociously that they write for children only: William Mayne 'because it is the only sensible thing to do', Alan Garner because 'it imposes a literary discipline, a compulsion to find a language that will bring all the complexity of the reality children share with adults within the verbal and conceptual compass of the young'. P. L. Travers, not new but still going very strong with that—to me—rather unalluring witch Mary Poppins, says she writes for children because she respects their eyesight. They find visible 'the ill-defined area between the possible and the impossible, fantasy and unreality . . . the gap between the first and last strokes of midnight at the end of one year and the beginning of another that is soldered over for adults.' 'I talk about myth,' she says . . . 'It is like talking to the cosmos.' But she agrees—and so of course must the others—that no book which children like, even if the author says it is written for children only, is much good if it is *liked* by children only. C. S. Lewis said long ago that books written for children only are by definition bad books.

Why one writes fiction at all of course one never knows or does well not to try to say. Novelists are usually and mercifully quiet about it. Among children's writers—who are, as I'm trying to indicate, on the whole a waspish lot since they have the unfortunate image of being thought, by people who don't know any, rather sweet—among children's writers, talking about ignition one remembers Carroll saying that he sent Alice off down the rabbit-hole without the faintest idea of what was going to happen to her (a statement that has excited Freudians for years): and Swift one remembers, speaking of the first glorious dawn over Lilliput, Nothing to it, says he, you think of big men and little men and you're away. And of R. L. Stevenson, who wrote *Treasure Island* because one wet day a boy was messing with chalks at a table. Stevenson sat down alongside and drew a map.

It is Sylvia Townsend Warner, the literary descendant of Swift, 'the Deaconess Swift' as Geoffrey Grigson calls her, who talks of wasps in marmalade. She is speaking in a collection of stories called *Kingdoms of Elfin*—all about fairies let me tell you—as cruel and brilliant and comic and furious and brave as wasps themselves. It is a book stripped clean of pity though it can bring tears. Such children as appear in it are regarded with a very steady eye. She cares as little as her characters about her audience. Maugré in this book, an elf, fears a slash which will slice him like a wasp in marmalade from the sword of a minister of the church of Scotland—a slash I may say he very much deserves. Maugré has read *The Secret Commonwealth* (known of course to Swift), written in 1691, and has heard that a second-sighted person like the minister has been known to cut the bodies of one of these elf-people in two with his iron weapon. Going too far, thinks Maugré, even for a legend and he proceeds to deal with the minister, occupying his house, watching him even in his dreams, stealing his baby and throwing it in the meal chest and then changing it for some frightful creature of his own. When the minister appears one day with such a look of calm and finality that the elf thinks he must have been murdering his wife, the elf proceeds to drive the man mad by the terrible method of a ceaselessly striking clock (bells of course in fiction are very reckless, cf. Iris Murdoch, Dorothy Sayers and *The Hunting of the Snark*)—causing the man at last to be taken off to the County Bridewell; his wife and children to go and live with her sister above a grocery shop in Glasgow.

A most terrible end.

I find the elvish world of Miss Townsend Warner a most thrilling discovery. Her creatures I think mark the end of a cycle, turning back to Swift and a more ancient supernatural. They nod in passing to Tolkien's brood of hobbits and suchlike, but to my mind they have wit and pace and character that far transcend them. Miss Townsend Warner's elves are tough nuts. They tend to be philosophers—logical positivists mainly; they discuss the Trinity; are often very well read. Christianity they find on the whole hilarious (though they love churches and architecture); humans are usually incomprehensible though they have areas of piercing sensitivity. Sexual passion can be most sweet, most painful, love affairs serious enough to last a hundred years. Manners are fastidious—only peasants fly or show their wings, but on the other hand monstrous births occur in all social classes, even princely. Monkeys are torn in half, cats dissected for pleasure. There is room enough for a glenful of Dunsinanes and some very odd alchemistic surgery. But conversation is always excellent and all elves good and evil, if there are such qualities as these here, tend to be very entertaining. Elves and humans regard each other warily, courteously, trying not to show any particular curiosity with rather the same formality it occurs to me as I tried to muster up

last year on the border of China watching Chinese farmers growing lettuces. Our manners were very good, but we were worlds
apart.

I think that *Kingdoms of Elfin* has crystallized all that Tolkien
and Lewis and their imitators have been doing these forty years
when they lifted the supernatural world out of a very spongy part
of the field. This book has nothing to do with children's literature
at all. The stories are mostly reprinted from *The New Yorker*.

The supernatural, that is to say the relating of myth and legend,
was in abeyance when I was growing up. Fantasy was rampant
but the imagination was much neglected. Elves for example
in the 'thirties were washy, wisp-like insects who never stopped
grinning or flying about.

Sometimes they shone lights and sniffled and got shut in chests
of drawers with shadows and died (ridiculous) if children did not
believe in them at pantomimes. They peeped at you archly round
the capital letters and chapter headings of fairy books. They had
ridiculous single whiskers growing up above their eyes. They
were about five inches high and flimsy, when, as everybody
knows and has known for twenty centuries, they have always
been several feet high with the muscles of stevedores. They scam-
pered at you out of harebells, they swung euphorically at you on
twigs: and I think that they did considerable damage, much more
damage than Enid Blyton. Enid Blyton's stories may have been
consolatory, but they are not of the same order as the emasculated
elf.

Some years ago I was transfixed with fright watching a television interview where a woman of about my age was being asked to
talk about her conviction that she was always seeing fairies. She
was a sensible woman, round faced, glasses, good shoes. She
looked rather upsettingly like me. 'Yes,' she said, 'I see them
most days. I first saw them at an evening lecture.'

'What were they like?' asked the interviewer.

'Oh, they were sweet. I was sitting at the lecture—it was at the
Women's Institute—beside a beautiful floral arrangement, and I
noticed that one of the flowers was broken. It was a Canterbury
Bell. And as I watched, a little fairy came along: and then some
other little fairies. They were dressed in green, with little blue-
bell hats on, and they began to stitch up the stalk—two of them
held the flower while two of them stitched. Such tiny little stit-
ches. I couldn't stop watching. I didn't listen to any more of the
lecture at all.'

'And you see these fairies often, Mrs Hookaneye?'

'Oh, yes. I see them almost every day now. They dance at night in the kitchen. All over my working surfaces. I see the marks of their little feet. I have made a little flap for them in my back door.'

Poor wretched woman.

But what is interesting is that these ninny creatures—the Tinkerbells and Mabel Lucy Atwells would have been spared her had it not been for the nonsense she had met with in the books and picture books of her youth. The old elves are best.

For myself—I first came upon children's literature through my Auntie Nellie, a rich woman who lived in nursing homes and who presented my brother and me when I was seven and he was three each with a china mug from which we drank milk at tea-time. I was an undersized child and so for some years this mug was at eye-level every day. I spent much time regarding it. The handle was the frightful tail of a fawn caterpillar, curling down and round the mug in low-relief, ending at the back in a patient face and a harness of clean cobwebs. On its back were being heaped all kinds of parcels by the familiar, flat, grasshopper synthetic elves in their blue-bell hats and the expressions of health visitors. Written beneath the cartoon were the words 'Something attempted something done has earned a night's repose'—a sentiment which has perhaps been the reason for my dread of finishing anything and a habit of wandering the house at night.

Across the table—and this was my real introduction to literature and because it was my brother's mug and not mine perhaps accounts for any waspishness of my own—across the table my brother's mug had as a handle a glorious, fat red robin with a glaring black eye and as legend—by some fine accident—the words 'A Robin Redbreast in a Cage Puts all Heaven in a Rage'. From that moment, not knowing his existence, I felt Blake to be a superlative children's poet and I have never changed my mind.

But apart from the mugs the literature on offer was very watery marmalade. I think that I was unfortunate in that neither of my parents seemed to have read anything as children and there were no thumbed or even unthumbed copies of Mrs Molesworth about the house or of Mrs Nesbit or of Frances Hodgson-Burnett. Worse, there were no Brothers Grimm, no Hans Andersen, no Andrew Lang. In 1936 my Auntie Nellie produced a book of songs by A. A. Milne—bears and honey jars, a Nannie in a flowing dress and huge apron that seemed archaic, a golden-haired little boy, much loved and rich, who wandered in summery spinneys in

Sussex (we lived on Teesside), hung thoughtfully over bridges and sweetly said his prayers. He had heart-breaking dents in the backs of his knees.

I reacted violently. A Maugré. If I had been able to get my hands in his hair he'd have been in the meal-chest. One look at Pooh and I was for wasps, not bees and honey. A vile, Iago-like child, I hated Christopher Robin 'because he hath a daily beauty in his life that makes me ugly'. I looked elsewhere.

And oh so few places to look. It seems extraordinary, our house was a schoolmaster's house but there were only three bookshelves. My father taught Mathematics and Physics and I don't think had ever read a novel. My mother was an Anglo-Catholic and all her books seemed to be by Dean Inge. There was no bookshop in the town, no public library, no library at my kindergarten or at the junior part of the High School to which I went when I was eleven. In the Senior School there was the County Library Cupboard, locked with a padlock, which contained forty books, changed at monthly intervals and unlocked for an hour on alternate Wednesdays. I went back to my old school three years ago to present the prizes there—I had written a book about it—a book which I had thought (modestly) like Dickens might cause the establishment to be closed down. But no. I was invited back and shown a library now of such splendour that I was humbled and shamed and decided that the bi-Wednesday cupboard must have been a myth. And it certainly seems a myth that through this cupboard, like Alice grabbing at the pot of marmalade as she fell, I achieved a place to read English Literature at length at the University and several happy years afterwards in the Reading Room of the British Museum.

A good part of the year however was spent during my father's long holidays at his father's farm in West Cumberland and here there were no books at all except the family Bible. It had a big metal clasp and when you opened it a waft of must blew out. The pages had fawn blobs on them and cauliflower and cumulus-shaped fungus but I read the Old Testament through. The New Testament I avoided. I think perhaps because there were so very many pictures of Jesus on the bedroom walls at home—Jesus robed like Christopher Robin's nannie, emasculated like an elf—for all I know even accompanied by an elf. Certainly all the saints about the house, mostly drawn—very prettily—by Margaret Tarrant, were in the company of rabbits. Saints were so frequently accompanied by rabbits in the 'thirties and 'forties that it is interesting to reflect upon whether this was a subconscious equivalent of the witch and her hare. About the same time you remember the Easter rabbit emerged and superseded the chicken. Most unnecessarily it seemed to me.

But the rabbit in English fiction is a massive subject—the sixteenth-century coney-catching pamphlet, you will remember, providing the very germ of the English novel. Rabbits have since troubled fiction through the centuries and exploded at last in the hugest rabbit book of all, a massive publishing phenomenon, *Watership Down*, read openly in trains by bankers and senior members of the Civil Service. Rabbits are mighty in fiction. I have no intention of embarking on them here.

The farm dining room where I had the luck to find the Old Testament was a very grand room in which I never remember eating a meal and could be quite alone. The table was covered with a furry carpet. There were mirrors and lustres and embroidered texts and the best china in a cabinet. Out of the window beyond the geraniums on the sill was Skiddaw mountain and across the room was a huge old court cupboard with 1691 carved on it—the year of *The Secret Commonwealth*—a cupboard so big that, we were always told, the new eighteenth-century farmhouse had been built round it. I used as a child to climb in through one of its lower doors and along inside and out the other end as if crawling down a tunnel. Tunnels, tunnels! Have no fear—my progress down the cupboard did not land me in marmalade; nor did I come out at the other end finding that there had been a timeslip and everybody was in mob caps or periwigs; nor did the back of the cupboard fall out and I find myself in a land of lions who were really God, and witches who were much less seductive than Satan. Nor did it lead me to the new, liberated children's fiction where the young do more advanced things in cupboards than their parents were allowed even to read about forty years ago at the dingier end of the dingier bookshops in the Charing Cross Road.

No. I crawled one summer's day through the dining-room cupboard at the farm where there had been for a long time a mouldy old heap of paper and I pulled a book out of the middle of it. It was a thin, cheap-looking book, its cardboard back bent up at the corners and the pages freckled and stuck together. It was called *Northanger Abbey* and I carried it about the farm and fields a good bit afterwards.

I should like to say that I read it. But I don't believe I did read much. I suppose I was a bit young for it if I was still crawling about in cupboards. But I do remember feeling something particular about it. The name seemed beautiful. I was very taken with the way the sentences went. My grandmother quickly took it from me anyway. She did not like to see time wasted out of doors reading.

The things in that cupboard she said were nothing. They had come from a neighbouring farm where there had been a murder. One of the farmer's daughters—the elder sister of a friend of mine— had been shot through the window by her lover, a soldier; and her body later decorated 'every bit over with wild flowers' by the squire's daughter who had once been a nurse—at what must have been a most leisurely hospital. The soldier was hanged at Durham gaol. He was said to be mentally retarded and went screaming to the gallows. We talked of it slowly and often round the kitchen fire in the evenings. The books had come, said my grandmother, from a tainted place. On no account was I to read *Northanger Abbey* for it might upset me.

For a long, long time afterwards—more years than I like to admit— I credited Jane Austen with a Hardyan quality not generally re- cognized and had to make an effort later in life not to associate her with violent death: *The Trumpet Major* or that terrible story, *The Melancholy Hussar*.

It would be fun to pretend that I let it be known to my agent when years and years afterwards I began to write fiction that I had had a Lake District childhood—an enormous advantage in a writer of children's books. The North West has been an ancient place for stories which children enjoy. Most of the stories cer- tainly are about people on very short visits. Sir Gawain in search of the Green Knight—somewhere round the Trough of Bowland if you remember—was glad to get home. Beowulf and his not par- ticularly merry men off after Grendel and his mother in what sounds very like Wastwater were much relieved to get back to base and start the party; and the ubiquitous Arthur seems to have been content to choose the North only for his mausoleum under Richmond castle—though his father, Pendragon, the cannibal of Castlethwaite, was resident and no weekender, in the very heart of things at Mallerstang. A gallop would have got him to Beatrix Potter by lunchtime and to Arthur Ransome for evening cocoa.

They are waspish these people, sometimes ferocious (not King Arthur) and stern with the young. 'When I was a little girl I was satisfied, with about six books,' says Beatrix Potter. 'I think chil- dren nowadays have too many.' Arthur Ransome, writing of the most blissful happiness of his own Lake District holidays as a boy, when in the Middle East and middle age, and he was operating so surprisingly as a secret service agent, seems not to have liked children at all.

My time in the Lake District was not a bit like that—no boats, no camps, no giants or knights in armour. We were all expected to work at the farm and get the harvest in. There were still—noticeably even to a child—the remains of the awful poverty of the 'twenties. Farmers in West Cumberland had recently been hungry. Life was still frugal. Farm servants were still called hinds, even in the 'forties. The women were 'hired-girls', often too poor to marry. Illegitimate children were usual and accepted and on arrival brought round from farm to farm by their grandmothers and given shillings like other new babies. There was most tremendous hard drinking. Language especially in the fields was rich and funny and foul—strong stuff for a schoolmaster's daughter whose mother read only Dean Inge. I have been eternally grateful for it. There had been this murder—and other things. A neighbouring farmer in his cups used to hunt his sons with a gun. Round a spinney where there was neither Pooh nor Eeyore. In winter, as in Laurie Lee's Gloucestershire at precisely this time 'in winter incest flourished where the roads were bad'. It was a long way from *Swallows and Amazons*. In fact in whispering distance sometimes of *Cold Comfort Farm*.

But not such a great way from Beatrix Potter. Even before the days of Auntie Nellie's milk mug I had met her—literally met her—because my mother discovering Squirrel Nutkin in a shop in York when she was on a Mother's Union outing, deserted Dean Inge at last and proceeded to Sawrey, which was not far from our farm. I remember a little, bent, sideways-glancing person looking at me over a gate and a sense of toughness and purposefulness of a high order. I was being led along by a hand—my mother's—and high above me was my mother's face, pink with pleasure at seeing the bunny lady.

She was no bunny lady to me. That she put rabbits in trousers worried me not a bit. They were real rabbits often ridiculous and vicious, and real trousers the sort that ought to be spelt with a W—trowsers. There was ruthlessness in the text as well as the heavenly beauty of the pictures and the sense of immense trouble taken. Look for instance at the drawing of the cat trussed up with string in the *Tale of Samuel Whiskers*, ready to be rolled in pastry. Nobody I think could draw a cat trussed up with string, like breast of lamb with stuffing, without a model. I believe that Beatrix Potter trussed up that cat. She drew it, and its anguished

face is a portrait, the portrait of a cat whose relationship with its
owner was to say the least a little odd. It is the world of Maugré
and the Scottish minister. I believe that Miss Potter could have
dealt with Miss Townsend Warner's Winged Creatures and by
the gleam of her eye, needing no Iron Weapon.

I doted and I dote upon Beatrix Potter especially when she is
murky—the terrible house of Mr Tod, the awful wet, dark, Lake
District afternoon leaden through the windows, the slate, the
dripping trees, the fearful smell of decay, the awful teeth of the
badger lying on the bed with the dreadful gallows bucket above
him. Years later in a lecture to do with Old Norse at the University I awoke to hear the lecturer likening the atmosphere of
Beowulf to Mr Tod's cottage. Among new writers both William
Mayne and Alan Garner who live in the emptier places of the
North and do not visit only for their summer holidays evoke this
atmosphere sometimes equally powerfully.

I wonder if it could happen now that a child in what was called
an educated home and at the best school in the district taught by
women with good degrees and whose only small talent was for
telling stories could have read so few? The enormous change
that has taken place since Tolkien began to give readings to his
friends of the first drafts of *Lord of the Rings* after dinner at
Merton while it is said the bombs were falling on London, the
book which C. S. Lewis said was 'like lightning from a clear sky':
the new availability of books, the excellence of most children's
libraries and the people believing in and promoting them, forming groups to urge children's imaginations on would have had
children like me as their prime target. I think however—though I'm
not saying that it would have been any loss except to my own
happiness—that such a barrage of kindness might have stopped me
from writing anything myself. Children's books are now so good,
so scholarly, so special, I think children may now react sometimes
as I did to Christopher Robin, and turn instead to Richmal
Crompton's *William*. They still can. There are new editions and
he has lately been on television of a Sunday afternoon, deathless
in his own way as Billy Bones. He has the weird formality that
children have—which Ivy Compton-Burnett so understood in children. She and Richmal Crompton were both classical scholars.
Though I think that in this august chamber each of them might
be surprised to be compared to the other! William is earnest, logical, dirty, maddening and hare-brained. He is not entirely without interest in 'the roots of existence' but he will never be 'cap-

tured by the forces of evil'. And if he goes through the back of a cupboard it is because he has broken it.

He is also—which some of the new didactic writers forget about children—hilariously funny. Children like to see themselves as funny. The best sound in the world is a child by itself laughing out loud at a book. I see the solemn faces of children sometimes brooding over *Lord of the Rings* or *Red Shift* and I feel rather sorry for them. Children need a lot of nonsense. They even need a lot of time to be without books at all. I think if I were a child now I would have disregarded all the delectable literature spread out for me and me alone, and on Puffin Club days in Church Street, Kensington I should have been the child who stayed at home rolled up in bed with the *Beano*, which thank goodness, like William, is still about.

I should have felt like Gavin Ewart in a poem in a recent number of the *Times Literary Supplement* called 'My Children's Book':

> In my book even the jokes will be bad
> Everyone will live in a state of disgrace
> And have misadventures. No angels or fairies
> Will be able to stand the atmosphere for more than a minute
> Real life of any kind will seem a blessed relief.

Or perhaps not. Perhaps all this fiction of the golden age of the children's book would have slowed me up and left me stuck in the marmalade for ever. The great pity of the new children's fiction is that it is cut off from the rest of fiction at least until it is about thirty years old—it has special reviewers, special sections in the literary journals as well as in the bookshops and the libraries. On television book programmes, if it is Children's Books night, you will see that the chairman of the panel has a special sort of face like an uncle at a birthday party waiting for the home-going balloons, the restorative gin and tonic.

Writers of children's books sometimes understandably deal with this by a rather dotty arrogance, refusing to read any other literature themselves, relentlessly reviewing only each other ('incest flourishes where the roads are bad'), becoming at last pathetic people, ever feebler and finally are deep in the marmalade unable even to twitch.

I like to think such few books as I have done have nothing to do with new directions in children's literature; but then I suppose no writer of fiction ever admits a precise debt, unless (I notice) it is in one of their books they don't like (Iris Murdoch when she is told you never did anything like the first, *Under the Net*—the thing you should never say—replies that this book is the most derivative).

I like, of course, some of what P. L. Travers says about children's eyesight; but I could never talk to the cosmos. Quite beyond me. Similarly for all my awe of Alan Garner I could never do the homework of getting my characters to unlock the power of the past. And I cannot at present even write about violence. And sex is tentative, suggested and not gymnastic. Politics I cannot cope with at all. I have never I hope written a word meant to ennoble or to educate. And although I almost worship *Kingdoms of Elfin* as I almost worship Swift I don't suppose I shall ever write about tearing monkeys in half. 'One writes what one can, not what one should,' says Iris Murdoch.

I can only write very tame tales, mostly about the tragi-comedy of being young. I sometimes even sing of vicars's daughters. If people read them, and particularly if they sometimes laugh at them, I could not ask for any more.

'Now William,' said his mother anxiously at lunch, 'you'll go to the dancing class nicely this afternoon won't you?'

'I'll go the way I gen'rally go to things,' said William.

'I've only got one way of goin' anywhere. I don't know whether it's nice or not.'

ARTIST UPON OATH

ROBERT GITTINGS, CBE, LITT D, FRSL

Read 26 February 1976:
John Guest, MA, FRSL, in the Chair

IT is in the second half of our century that Biography has come of age, in this country at least. If statistics mean anything, it was announced a few years ago that the number of biographical books published annually in this country had for the first time topped the thousand mark. Any librarian will say how the stock and borrowings of non-fiction have increased, and much of this, apart from technical know-how and do-it-yourself books, is likely to be in biography. The size of the biography shelves in any local or public library also indicates this. Academically, as always, recognition of biography as a separate form, rather than as an adjunct to history or to literature, has come more slowly. Though I stand to be corrected here, I know of only one thoroughly well-established course of undergraduate studies solely in English Biography, and that is in Boston University, where I had the great pleasure of teaching it just over five years ago, to a class with which it was reckoned a normal and valuable part of literature.

This is natural, since biography in English has a short history compared with most other literary arts; it is still under 500 years old; so the short survey, with which I want to begin this talk, in tracing its history, will not take long. Of course, there were what might be called biographies, written in Latin, throughout the earlier history of this country, but I do not think they qualify. For one thing, most of them were not strictly biography, but hagiography. They were written solely to glorify or commemorate the subject of the great man they celebrated, and they were always written about great and important public figures. They were limited in other ways. They were a mixture of personal knowledge, usually by some subordinate or official, and a kind of guesswork. Therefore, where the author was working in this sphere of personal knowledge, they could often be sound and accurate; where they ventured outside, into other aspects of the subject's life, they were often nonsensical. Asser, bishop of Sherborne, wrote a life of King Alfred, in whose household he had been, in the ninth century. As one would expect from a cleric, this is good on Alfred's scholarship and love of learning, with first-hand anecdotes about the King as a translator and pioneer of education. Where Asser falls down is on the King as a general, because, having been a monk, he knew nothing about fighting. He gets all the military tactics of Alfred's battles against the Danes completely back to front. And, like all these early works, it is official history; the sole personal touch is that he suggests Alfred had piles, an occupational hazard of scholars. Eadmer, another monk in the early twelfth century, wrote a similar life of Anselm. He stresses his holy life, piety, fasts, vigils, miracles, the running of a monastery, all those things he knew about; he has one or two personal anecdotes, some charming, some strange. Anselm, it appears, had the power to see through the walls of the monastery, so as to tell what the other monks were doing in their cells, a most uncomfortable gift in a Father Superior. This is all very well but of Anselm, the statesman, the companion of Kings, he says nothing because he knows nothing. There is a certain amount of dubious history, but far more of relics and wonders associated with Anselm after death than his effect on England and the State when he was alive.

These pious and partial lives are all we get in this line until biography really begins, and biography in English too, with Sir Thomas More's life of Richard III, written about 1513. Lately, there has been a move to treat this not as the first example of biography, but the first great propaganda exercise in blackening a past regime so as to gratify the present order. If so—and I'm not sure it was so—it misfired. More, as all biographers should be, was too honest a man. He used a lot of first-hand information, mostly, it must be admitted from people favoured by the new Tudor regime; to that extent he was biased. Yet More, as we all know, hated tyranny of all sorts. His Richard III may well be a warning to his own master, Henry VIII, not to let his own reign get out of hand; and that may be why it was never printed in his lifetime, and indeed was left unfinished. It was followed in the middle of

the sixteenth century by two lives, that of More himself by his
son-in-law Roper, and of Wolsey by his gentleman-usher George
Cavendish. Both, in their way, still share the character of these
eulogistic lives of the Middle Ages. They come to praise, and
praise only: both have a set, old-fashioned wheel-of-fortune pattern: the rise and fall of a great man. Cavendish also shows the
lack of proportion of earlier chronicles. Wolsey's later days, when
Cavendish knew him, take up one-third of the whole. Yet biography is progressing, in honesty, thoroughness, its attempt to
show a whole man.

The next is a leap forward, with Isaac Walton. His biographies
are the very first that are pieces of conscious literary art. The
biographer is now an artist; though, as in my title, an artist upon
oath. Walton's *Lives*—of Donne, Hooker, Herbert, Wotton, San-
derson—might not pass the tests of modern biography. They still
look back to the medieval tradition of 'saintly' biographies,
though now the saints have to be High Anglican, and they are in
that predominately religious. For example, the literary side of
Donne is hardly even mentioned. Yet these are biographies written by a person, not just a pious recorder. Walton is individual,
even in the tricks he plays on the reader, inventing imaginary
dialogues 300 years in advance of Lytton Strachey doing it, holding up the action by long digressions, from which Walton disarm-
ingly returns with 'but now I return to my account' or even in
one instance, 'but now I return from my long digression'. But
believable, human characters are beginning to appear, caught in
unofficial and domestic poses, such as the picture that delighted
Keats so much of Hooker rocking his child's cradle.

John Aubrey, who follows in his *Brief Lives*, has often been
criticized for being too domestic, and too unbelievably and tri-
vially anecdotal. I do not altogether agree. Admittedly, Aubrey
hardly ever finished anything he set out to do; but he was far
from being the silly old potterer in a seventeenth-century dress-
ing-gown we have come to visualize through a recent brilliant
one-man stage adaptation of his *Lives*. He had a sharp eye, a shar-
per ear for dialogue, and though garrulous himself could get
other people to talk. Now we really have people as they were, in
their minor as well as major moments, and I don't mean the
endlessly-repeated bawdy incidents, such as Sir Walter Raleigh
and the susceptible Maid of Honour. And talking of that, women
are for the first time presented as themselves, not just as the
wives, daughters or mistresses of the heroes of biography, but
with real appreciation of their personal qualities: as in his own

words about the Countess of Warwick, 'She needed neither bor-
rowed shades nor reflexive lights to set her off.'

About the time that Aubrey wrote, the second half of the seventeenth century, literary biography is attempted, that difficult
art of relating the man to the work. Sprat's life of the poet
Cowley connects the poet's *reading* with his own *writing*, and the
principle of this is enunciated by Dr Johnson in the next century.
In a letter to Thomas Warton junior in 1754, on the subject of
Warton's book on Spenser's *Faerie Queene*, Johnson wrote:

> You have shown to all who shall hereafter attempt the study
> of our ancient authors the way to success by directing them to
> the perusal of the books those authors had read.

Those who criticize and stigmatize what they call 'source-hunt-
ing' in literary biography should realize that it has a sound history of nearly 300 years, and weighty sanction. Johnson himself,
of course, was no mean biographer; but it is with Boswell *on*
Johnson that modern biography comes to birth. We now know
enough about Boswell himself to see that the old idea of him
merely as a hovering, importunate note-taker is quite false. He
faced and met successfully nearly all the problems of a modern
biographer. First, he corrected former biography, that of Sir
John Hawkins. Then, he did not use solely personal knowledge,
but genuine research into the fifty-four years of Johnson's life
before Boswell even met him. He wove this research so skilfully
with personal knowledge that the life has a sense of proportion.
He used judgment and above all commonsense; he is an analyst,
not just a recorder. He employs and weighs several sources of
evidence for one incident, and he refutes gossip. He adds—and here
the artist takes over from the researcher—the conciseness and accu-
racy his own legal training had taught him; a genuine love of the
subject and personal sympathy; total frankness, learnt, we now
realize, from his own self-analysis in his own journals; most important, a full sense of background—Goldsmith, Garrick, Reynolds,
and even minor figures are all characters in their own right; and
he understood the seriousness of his subject. His immense sense
of fun is never at the expense of Johnson's own stature. Though
of its time—and I suspect he caught some of his story-telling knack
from Roger North's delightful biography of his brother John
North—it is a biography for all time.

Unfortunately, nineteenth-century biography did not live up to
Boswell. Carlyle in his essay 'On Boswell' might proclaim, 'History is the new poetry', but he and others showed a false poetry in

their disregard of facts. One poet, Robert Southey, in his life of Nelson, wandered so far as to say that Nelson's love of Lady Hamilton 'did not, in reality, pass the bounds of ardent and romantic admiration'. Influenced both by Carlyle himself, and by evangelical piety, the biographer's subject became once more the infallible hero, not the fallible but lovable man of Boswellian biography. There were some most honourable exceptions, such as Mrs Gaskell's life of Charlotte Brontë, fighting for the truth in spite of relatives and friends; but the pious and, it must be said, immensely long biography became the sacred cow, which Lytton Strachey, in our century, set himself to slaughter. Not that Strachey, it seems to me, really achieved anything new. For the pious rhetoric of the Victorians, he simply substituted a Bloomsbury snigger. He also betrayed some of the first principles of biography. He hardly ever, if ever, used first-hand sources; his *General Gordon* is based mainly on the most dubious third-hand accounts. His style is often a distortion of the facts. In the best of his *Eminent Victorians*, that on Florence Nightingale, the fact that 'she used to nurse and bandage the dolls her sister damaged' becomes with Strachey 'Her sister had shown a healthy pleasure in tearing her dolls to pieces.' One of the commonest fallacies is that Freudian analysis came in with Strachey, and biography has never been the same since. I think we now see that it was a matter of substituting one set of symbols for another, though I delight in learning from a very fine analytical biography of Kenneth Grahame that Toad, in *The Wind in the Willows*, with his splendid waistcoats and even more splendid cheek to the magistrate, is really subconsciously Oscar Wilde.

But I am not going to particularize the many fine biographies which have been written over the last twenty-five years, in what I have called the coming-of-age of English biography. For one thing, there are too many biographers present; though I hope those who are here will recognize what I shall now say about their work and their art. It seems to me that things have happened in our time. These are, to generalize, a widening of our ideas about what constitutes a life, and a widening of the means to express that life accurately and fully. In terms of my title, the biographer as an artist now compasses a far larger area of human experience; as a witness upon oath he or she has now many more means of insuring that what is written is as near as possible to the truth.

Our conception of what should be encompassed in a life is infinitely larger than it was fifty or even twenty-five years ago. At the same time, though this may seem a paradox, it is infinitely

neater, shorter and to the point. This was, in fact, Strachey's real
contribution; he kept it short and stylistically interesting, like the
artist he was. We no longer—or hardly ever—have biographies that
begin by going back to the Norman Conquest, in which a nineteenth-century character called, shall we say, Pugwash, has to have
his genealogy traced from 'one Sir Brian de Piggewashe'. Nor do
we usually now have what used to be very popular earlier in this
century, the kind of approach adopted in the translated biographies of Emil Ludwig, where we are given a guided tour of all the
contemporary events in Europe, or even the world, before a baby—
who turns out to be, say, Napoleon Buonaparte—gets himself born.
You still do get this kind of thing occasionally, an example of
which I hope I may quote without parody: such as this.

On the morning of 11 December 1846, as the 28 gun frigate
HMS Rattlesnake slipped westward down the Channel from
Plymouth, the world had spun on its orbit for some 4500 million years. On its surface dwelt nearly 1500 million human
beings. No less than 450 million of them lived among the
crumpled brown folds of China. Another 180 million swarmed
on the sub-continent of India. Some 70 million were spread
across the plains of the Russian Empire. From Britain, a small
island off the North West coast of Europe, fewer than 28 million people ruled one-sixth of the world.

To do him justice, one can see what the author is getting at; some
sort of global view of biography. Yet that is not the large view of
a man which, I suggested, is the mark of modern biography. It is
large in a purely external way. What is so striking about present-
day biography is its large view of an individual man or woman's
interests and activities. It studies and considers every possible
influence on, and every possible aspect of, its subject. It is not
just biography concerned with the subject's professional or personal life only. It calls for much wider understanding than that.
Literary biography is not merely the subject's literary life; an
engineer's biography is not just concerned with technique or even
the history of engineering. Modern biography admits everything
that may influence or connect itself with the subject. This puts a
tremendous onus on the biographer. Once you allow that you
must write about the whole life, you let in everything that may
have impinged on that life. A thorough mastery of engineering
problems is only part of what you must achieve for your study of
the engineer. A thorough appreciation of poetry is only halfway
in your study of the poet. We need more than, in Johnson's

words, 'a perusal of the books those authors had read'. We need
to know as well what architecture, what paintings, what scenery
they saw, what social and political ideas they discussed, where
and how they travelled, what physical or psychological illnesses
they suffered from: what theatres, art galleries, concerts, sporting
events they attended—everything, in fact, that did or could have an
effect on them.

This would at first seem an impossible task to achieve fully. To
write a biography would be the literary equivalent of a life sentence; the word 'life' would take on a most sinister meaning. Yet,
very fortunately, the modern biographer has aids to what I called
a widening of the means to express that life fully and accurately. I
do not mean by that the many mechanical aids to research, mic-
rofilm, photo copies, xeroxes, computers, and so on. These certainly speed up the methods of finding and assembling facts, but
they are not in themselves a whole answer to the biographer's
needs. They are often unsatisfactory for a whole mass of older
documents, and they often do not give a sound method of comparison between several sources at the same time. Many biographers will say that there is nothing like having a whole collection
of manuscripts spread out on a nice large table, so that the eye
can pass easily from one to another. We tend too to think of biographer's evidence as primarily manuscript; whereas it contains
so many more forms of evidence. The means I meant are all the
local and specialized museums, collections, libraries and record
offices: museums and libraries of medical history, for example,
institutes of art and art history, theatre museums, specialized scientific collections, industrial archaeology. One of the great aids in
the last twenty-five years at least has been the growth and ex-
tensive use of local record offices. Not only have they themselves
had better staffing, better handling and preserving facilities, but
it has been far more widely recognized, sometimes almost for the
first time, that they are places worthy of receiving archives of
family, business, personal or technical material. The modern biographer will get immense help from the special and often surprising resources of the local or specialized collection all over the
country.

The large public and national collections have also improved,
though they, very often, had a long way to go, according to biographers working in them well within living memory. Early in
this century, for example, Sir Sidney Colvin employed for his
biography of John Keats a research assistant for a particular purpose. This was to untangle the Chancery law-suit, in which a

good deal of Keats's money was involved, and Colvin's assistant
was a lawyer. Yet even he was defeated, not only by the cataloguing system at the Public Record Office, but by the fact, as he
writes ruefully and amusingly to Colvin in letters now at Keats
House, that the room at the Public Record Office was so dark—it
was in the depths of winter—and that no one there would provide
artificial light, so that in some days he had to give up work almost
as soon as he started. I made some enquiries about this lack of
provision of artificial light at the P.R.O., and was told a tradition—
how true I do not know—that the attendants deliberately withheld
from visitors any form of lighting, and when all the researchers
had gone, early and frustrated, the attendants would get out their
Government candles, and play cards by them till the official clos-
ing time. As I say, I do not know the truth of that, and certainly
there was enough light when I did the same work a dozen years
ago; but even then the cataloguing was formidable, since all documents in a case are left under their original Chancery heads; and
since the whole Chancery system, as we know from Dickens, was
devised so that the public should never know what was going on,
this constitutes a severe handicap. One distinguished American
biographer of Keats, I know, looked at the Chancery indexes and
walked out, never to return there.

Still, generally now, the biographer has immense aids to research, which former ages have lacked. Even so, the task is formidable, not so much for the quantity, but even more for a certain quality it demands. The quality I mean is sympathy, imaginative and yet accurate sympathy, with every branch of life. One
has literally to live *with* the subject, to go exactly the same steps
as the subject. Technical and intellectual mastery is not enough.
Keats, in his famous definition of a poet, or rather the kind of
poet he felt himself to be, said that the poet had to be a chameleon, taking the exact colour of everything he lighted upon in the
way of experience. I would say that the biographer, in our definition, and in the demands of modern biography, has to be the
chameleon biographer. He or she must turn the colour of everything that life touches. 'Great and unobtrusive' was also what
Keats said a poem should be; the biographer's method should be
also great but unobtrusive. We should welcome, in most modern
work, the cessation of all that academic shadow-play of argument
with former writers on the subject, which used to disfigure biography. One is simply there to serve the subject, as best one can,
not to score points, or make what are academically called 'discoveries'—as if one could hope ever to discover more than a fraction of

the hidden life of any person. Such contests should be left to appendices or footnotes, their appropriate place. Where they are not, the effect can be ludicrous, and this still sometimes occurs. In a book on Browning, lately, a host of former authorities had somehow invaded the main text, so that they seemed to jostle the love-affair of Robert and Elizabeth, and even to be sharing their lives, while, to add to absurdity they were all given their full academic titles. This had the consequence that the privacy of Elizabeth Barrett's sick-room in Wimpole Street seemed suddenly invaded by the presence of a Sub Dean Emeritus.

It will have occurred to you, though, that to avoid the parading of argument is very far from avoiding argument altogether. This is inevitable in certain aspects of life. One of these is the aspect, in which, we are often told, biographers and their public in this century have become notably liberated and open-minded; and this is the sexual side of their subject, which, since we are admitting every aspect of life as the province of the biographer, must play a large part. I'm afraid I can't agree, though, that this has all become easy and plain in our time, as if by the waving of Strachey's phallic wand. It remains an extraordinary enigma, and especially its reception by public and critics, about which it is impossible to generalize. In fact, in dealing with it at all now, I shall take advantage of that most helpful part of my general briefing for this whole series of lectures on Innovations in Literature, which suggests I can draw on my own experience as a biographer. Here then, emphasizing that this is only my own experience in the biographies I have written, and regarding this, if you like as some sort of halfway interlude, is what I found happening; I can assure you that I am 'upon oath' in this too.

First, the biographer will always find that, in the minds of critics and public, there is always a pre-conceived idea about this side of the subject's life. When I first started trying to write about Keats, twenty-five years ago, I found there was a fairly widespread idea that Keats had had no sexual experience at all. This, in the face of many expressions in his own letters, and, as I came to find, in the drafts of poems, seemed unlikely, and I wondered how the idea came about. It could be traced, almost entirely, to someone I mentioned earlier, Sir Sidney Colvin. Colvin had an obsession about removing any sign of sex from any authors he dealt with. The Widener Library at Harvard contains evidence of Colvin's extraordinary treatment of the letters of Robert Louis Stevenson, pasting over with almost impenetrable gum, Stevenson's accounts of his sexual adventures in the South Seas.

With Keats, Colvin refused to the end of his life to print in his edition of Keats's letters any of the letters to Fanny Brawne, with their intense undercurrent of sexuality, though the words are decorous enough. With less decorous words in Keats's letters Colvin had the same principle: don't print. Saying he was omitting anything of what he called 'mere crudity', he went meticulously through, in a way which, paradoxically, has been of great help to a later biographer. Keats's original letters, now mostly at Harvard, sometimes have illegible words, written in haste; sometimes they are copies, by friends, who left words out which they could not read. Above these blanks or words, when I examined the letters, were scribbles in pencil; and after a good deal of comparison, I identified the hand of these pencil markings as that of Colvin himself. Further comparison revealed the words which Colvin had written in. What these did was to supply or complete a bawdy joke or phrase which Keats had made, and with which it was abundantly clear Colvin himself was quite familiar; only having completed it, he then invariably cut out the whole passage. I may say that this weird procedure was not solely confined to sex; Colvin condemned as his 'mere crudity' Keats's uncomplimentary outbursts about the higher clergy, such as when he called the Bishop of Lincoln 'a smashed frog putrefying'. That went out with the bawdy jokes too; in fact Colvin's editorial motto seems to have been No Bishop, No Sex.

At all events, his work left behind a formidable impression; and knowing that impression, I went somewhat carefully about my first biographical work on Keats. I only really suggested that, on the evidence, Keats had been quite naturally sexually attracted by two very beautiful young women at the same time. To my amazement and concern, I later found out the effect this had on one distinguished critic. According to his own biographer, it darkened the last years of his life; it obsessed the entries in his private diary; and—I have this on impeccable authority—he wrote to every other critic, who had approved of my book, to try and get them to retract and withdraw their judgments. Nor did it end there, nor with him. When I was preparing a much later biography of Keats, I got letters from people high in what one might call the Keats world, saying, in a hardly veiled way, that if I took a certain line on Keats and sex, I must expect bad reviews. Of course, I simply went ahead on what seemed to me the evidence, but I had had my warning. If there is this sort of preconception about your subject, it is dangerous to disprove it.

This was one reason, though only one, why I welcomed turning as a biographer from Keats to Hardy. It seemed that I could here tell the truth and please people. As many of you know, ten years ago a book came out purporting to show that Thomas Hardy had an illegitimate child by a sixteen-year-old girl, a child he never mentioned, provided for, or saw, and who was brought up by the girl's family. A lot of the argument seemed fallacious, and when I found a collection of letters of the girl's family, it seemed certain that this child never existed. I said so in my book. To my amazement once more, I found that with certain critics and readers, it was just as unpopular to say that Hardy didn't have this sexual experience, as it had been to say that Keats did have his experiences. Clearly, they wanted Hardy to have the bastard child. A most distinguished critic, who had complained publicly that there were no good Hardy critics, admitted that I seemed to have disproved the child; but still, he added that it 'felt right' that Hardy should have a bastard.

Even putting aside the odd idea that a biographer should lay down all responsibility, and insert into his book whatever 'feels right' to him, my efforts with Keats and Hardy left a puzzling situation. Searching for some general principle, I came up with one possible one. It was that, in England anyway, sex is bad in the town and good in the country. Keats was popularly supposed to be a cockney, Hardy a countryman—neither quite the whole truth, but that was the popular idea. It was therefore just as wrong and sordid for Keats to have sexual experience in Town, as it was right and even romantic for Hardy to have this suppositious sexual experience in the country. It was something to do, I thought, with the illusion of every English man and woman that they are really country folk, rooted in the land, just as so many urban American families still have the illusion of themselves as pioneer folk. This seemed, I must admit, a fanciful solution, but I was not at the end of my surprises. I had thought that Hardy himself, who knew if anyone did the actual sordid conditions of Dorset village and peasant life, conditions exposed in a set of special articles in *The Times* during Hardy's childhood—I should have said that Hardy himself would not have this illusion. Yet, just after this conclusion of mine, I found a passage I had missed in his own autobiography, which stated plainly that this verdict on Town and Country and sex was exactly his also. He wrote, in fact, this:

Rural life may reveal coarseness of considerable leaven; but that libidinousness which makes the scum of cities so noxious is not usually there.

So there we must leave it: who am I to go against the critics, the public, *and* Thomas Hardy? I can only point out again that every word I have just said is literally the truth, upon oath.

I hope you will forgive that perhaps rather light-hearted interlude—forgive it both for itself and even for being light-hearted—though I can only say in excuse that, while it is a doubtful proposition that truth is stranger than fiction, it seems almost self-evident that truth is usually funnier than fiction. However that may be, my real excuse is that I am now led to a tragic element in biography. For if biography is to deal with the whole of life fully, it must also deal fully with death, and very often of the effect on the personality of fatal illness or the treatment of that illness. This is a view put forward most persuasively by the medical historian Dr Hugh L'Etang, illustrated in his own fascinating miniature biographies of the great leaders of political life in this century, and I think it is true. It poses one of the most exacting problems for a biographer, especially problems of technical knowledge and judgment which are, speaking for myself, beyond many of us. You will guess that this applies particularly to any biographer of Keats, who has to take him right up to his appalling death from tuberculosis at the age of only twenty-five years and a few months. It is a thought which, without exaggeration, overshadows all the writing of that biography: how to treat the final chapter of Keats's life. As it grew nearer, I turned for guidance, as one must do all the time, to the many fine previous biographers. It was evident from their work that they had all felt the strain, and this appeared in all their final chapters. The most extreme were those who virtually omitted to have this final narrative. I am thinking, among others, of the splendid two-volume work by the late Professor Claude Finney. Finney's volumes are indeed entitled *The Evolution of Keats's Poetry*; but they do deal very fully with biographical matters. Yet Finney when he gets to that last tragic year of Keats's life, from his first haemorrhage to his death just over a year later, simply stops. He has the excuse that Keats wrote virtually no poems in that last year; but I think the reason is a different one. My guess is that Finney, a sensitive and compassionate man, and one of whom I was very fond, simply couldn't face writing about those months up to death. Indeed, no one can, who really imagines them: the young poet, with a disease which at that time was more or less incurable, dying miserably in a foreign land, in Rome, after a journey he should never have undertaken. When you read Keats's good and sensitive biographers—and there are many of them—you begin to feel how this oppresses them. One sign is a reaction they nearly all have in common. Instead of writing realistically about Keats in that miserable, diseased little room over the Spanish Steps, they take relief in loving descriptions of the beauties of the Roman landscape. I am not criticizing them in any way for this; it is perhaps the natural reaction, and it is an almost universal one. Of course, these beautiful prose sentences about the eternal city do incidentally throw into contrast the sick-room scene; but that is not the same as imaginatively partaking in what it meant to the desperate young poet, who had actually packed a large bottle of laudanum before he sailed, with the exact intention of committing suicide if his condition came to this: who knew, as a qualified doctor, with four close relatives already dead from the disease, that it would come to this. To try and show this, was one of my own most difficult tasks as a biographer.

Of course, in some ways it was bound to fail, as all biography must fail in such a situation; nor did some of my attempts to enter fully into that situation please everyone. I have been aware, from some public statements in other people's lectures, that I am supposed not to have done justice to Joseph Severn, the friend of Keats, who shared those last months. Now, any criticism of Severn as a fit companion for the dying poet was not made by me. It was made by Keats's doctor when the pair of them first arrived in Rome. The doctor said that Keats

> has a friend with him who seems very attentive to him but between you & I is not the best suited for his companion, but I suppose poor fellow he had no choice.

What I had to do as biographer was to paint the whole set of circumstances, and in particular, to interpret the doctor's remark that Severn was 'not the best suited for his companion'. I think I found the solution; and it was this. If you have ever nursed a mortally ill person, you know that, among all else, you have to be neat, efficient, and quick. It is so now, with all modern aids, and hundred times more so then. Any amount of good will can be negatived by lack of those qualities. If you read the unpublished and fragmentary autobiography of Severn himself, one fact in this innocent and self-revealing document sticks out like a sore thumb. The man himself was, as we should now say, absurdly accident-prone. Incidents showing this run all through his life. He cannot hammer a nail without driving it deeply into his flesh. He cannot boil water without scalding himself severely. In middle age, and when a father, he went to fetch his children from

a party. Passing along the road, he saw them, from over the
hedge, playing in their friend's garden. With the perpetual boyish
enthusiasm, which was both his charm and his downfall, he vaul-
ted the hedge. Unfortunately, he had not realized there was a line
of iron railings concealed on the other side, on which he impaled
himself vitally, and from which he had to be rescued with much
embarrassment—one can imagine the feelings of his own children.
Severn himself makes it clear in a letter that this kind of thing
went on in his devoted but muddled nursing of Keats. He
wrote:

> What enrages me most is making a fire. I blow-blow—for an
> hour—the smoke comes fuming out—my kettle falls over on the
> burning sticks—no stove—Keats calling me to be with him—
> the fire catching my hands & the door bell ringing—all these to
> one quite unused and not at all capable—

Now, this is a very human picture. It is comic, yes, but it is the
most tragic comedy. It partly makes intelligible actions by Keats,
such as his hurling away the cups of coffee Severn brought him—
Keats, the most efficient of young doctors, who had himself
nursed, with exemplary patience and professional care, his own
younger brother, from whom he had caught the fatal disease.
This tragi-comic juxtaposition strikes me as the real stuff of life,
certainly the stuff of an all-embracing, modern biography. And if
someone asks, what has this to do with Keats *as a poet*—and that,
after all, is why there is any biography of him in the first place—
there is a strikingly sufficient answer. During his short but amaz-
ingly mature life, Keats had evolved a philosophy, very like the
Christian belief, that only by losing your own life in the identity
of other people did you truly find yourself. It lies behind that
famous definition of the poet as a chameleon, taking colour from
everything he touches. It is also the point where *his* two iden-
tities, the life of a poet and the life of a physician, coincide, the
good doctor's sympathetic identification with his patient. Now, in
the final stages of illness, as I believe, it was this double identification that saved his last months from despair. Seeing that
Severn was in confusion and alarm at the visible signs of Keats's
coming death, Keats set himself to enter into Severn's identity,
and soften the blow for the puzzled and frightened young man.
'Did you ever see anyone die?' he asked Severn. 'No? Well,
then I pity you, poor Severn;' then, reassuring, 'now you must be
firm, for it will not last long'. Keats's whole poetic doctrine of
losing oneself in another's sufferings is contained in this and

similar remarks. He literally died, as he had lived, a poet; so his biographer can legitimately show him as a poet, up to his very last moment, and not abandon him when the actual written poetry ceases. One of his last sentences to Severn was 'Don't be frightened'—he was able to put Severn's fear before his own—and—as a doctor as well as poet—to say 'Don't breathe on me', in case Severn should catch the infection. It illustrates how the biographer has to be imaginatively and accurately in sympathy with his subject, even in those dying moments.

There are many other tasks for the biographer akin to these, tasks for which, in Keats's words, again on this subject of identification with others, one must be 'brave enough to volunteer for uncomfortable hours'. Perhaps in this talk I have sometimes emphasized too much the difficulties and vagaries of the calling. I should like to say how much it has its rewards, often emerging from those exact difficulties. There is the extraordinary sense of triumph, joy almost, when something that has been repeated again and again, the merest cliché, suddenly is seen to have real meaning in terms of character and human life. I almost think the highest example of this is something that has become one of the most-handled clichés in our history—those words spoken by H. M. Stanley: 'Dr Livingstone, I presume.' For over one hundred years a comedian's gag, it is astonishing how this remark can be rescued and made real by intelligent biography. The point was, as Stanley knew, Livingstone might simply not wish to be found. Touchy and suspicious, he was all too likely to dart off again and lose himself in the jungle, unless he was approached cautiously and tactfully. The tentative and deferential note Stanley adopted was the only way to win him over; and it led to something else of great human importance. Stanley's own youth and boyish diffidence came to remind the crotchety old man of his own son, with whom he had quarrelled, and about whom he was even now having guilty remorse. Getting to know him, he confessed how Stanley had, from the first, reminded him of his own boy, who had emigrated and died, in the American Civil War, in Stanley's own country. This meeting, far from being a parodist's picnic, was a moving and touching episode in the lives of both men.

In fact, it is through episodes such as this, treated skilfully by biography so that the characters of both men are fully developed, that one begins to guess one main way in which biography itself may be developing. I think the move is towards what may be called composite or group biography. One of the ways biography has already enlarged itself in this century is by paying more attention to the histories not only of the central character, but of all the people with whom he or she comes in contact. Whereas before, it was thought enough just to give thumb-nail sketches or short accounts of the facts about such characters, it has been seen that one needs a real appreciation of them, so as to judge their impact on, and interaction with, the character and work of the main subject.We have Keats's warning always, though:

> Above all, they are very shallow people who take everything literal. A Man's life of any worth is a continual allegory—and very few eyes can see the Mystery of his life . . . a life like the scriptures, figurative.

FEELING INTO WORDS

SEAMUS HEANEY

Read 17 October 1974:
John Press, MA, FRSL, in the Chair

I AM uneasy about speaking under the general heading of 'Innovation in Contemporary Literature': much as I would like to think of myself as breaking new ground, I find on looking at what I have done that it is mostly concerned with reclaiming old ground. My intention here is to retrace some of my paths into that ground, to investigate what William Wordsworth called 'the hiding places':

> the hiding places of my power
> Seem open; I approach, and then they close;
> I see by glimpses now; when age comes on,
> May scarcely see at all, and I would give,
> While yet we may, as far as words can give,
> A substance and a life to what I feel:
> I would enshrine the spirit of the past
> For future restoration.

To analyse the craft of putting feelings into words, is, inevitably, I think, to talk about poetry as divination, poetry as revelation of the self to the self, as restoration of the culture to itself; poems as elements of continuity, with the aura and authenticity of archaeological finds, where the buried shard has an importance that is not obliterated by the buried city; poetry as a dig, a dig for finds that end up being plants.

'Digging', in fact, was the name of the first poem I wrote

where I thought my feelings had got into words, or to put it more accurately, where I thought my *feel* had got into words. Its rhythms and noises still please me, although there are a couple of lines in it that have the theatricality of the gunslinger rather than the self-absorption of the digger. I wrote it in the summer of 1964, almost two years after I had begun to dabble in verses, and as Patrick Kavanagh said, a man dabbles in verses and finds they are his life. This was the first place where I felt I had done more than make an arrangement of words: I felt that I had let down a shaft into real life. The facts and surfaces of the thing were true, but more important, the excitement that came from naming them gave me a kind of insouciance and a kind of confidence. I didn't care who thought what about it: somehow, it had surprised me by coming out with a stance and an idea that I would stand over:

> The cold smell of potato mould, the squelch and slap
> Of soggy peat, the curt cuts of an edge
> Through living roots awaken in my head.
> But I've no spade to follow men like them.
>
> Between my finger and my thumb
> The squat pen rests.
> I'll dig with it.

As I say, I wrote it down ten years ago; yet perhaps I should say that I dug it up, because I have come to realize that it was laid down in me years before that even. The pen/spade analogy was the simple heart of the matter and *that* was simply a matter of almost proverbial common sense. As a child on the road to and from school, people used to ask you what class you were in and how many slaps you'd got that day and invariably they ended up with an exhortation to keep studying because 'learning's easy carried' and 'the pen's lighter than the spade'. And the poem does no more than allow that bud of wisdom to exfoliate, although perhaps the significant point in this context is that at the time of writing I was not aware of the proverbial structure at the back of my mind. Nor was I aware that the poem was an enactment of yet another digging metaphor that came back to me years later. This was a rhyme that also had a currency on the road to school, though again we were not fully aware of what we were dealing with:

> 'Are your praties dry
> And are they fit for digging?'
> 'Put in your spade and try,'
> Says Dirty-Face McGuigan.

Well, digging there becomes a sexual metaphor, an emblem of initiation, like putting your hand into the bush or robbing the nest, one of the various natural analogies for uncovering and touching the hidden thing. I now believe that the 'Digging' poem had for me the force of an initiation: the confidence I mentioned arose from a sense that perhaps I could work this poetry thing too, and having experienced the excitement and release of it once, I was doomed to look for it again and again.

I don't want to overload 'Digging' with too much significance. I know as well as you do that it is a big coarse-grained navvy of a poem, but it is interesting as an example—and not just as an example of what one reviewer called 'mud-caked fingers in Russell Square', for I don't think that the subject-matter has any particular virtue in itself—it is interesting as an example of what we call 'finding a voice'.

Finding a voice means that you can get your own feeling into your own words and that your words have the feel of you about them; and I believe that it may not even be a metaphor, for a poetic voice is probably very intimately connected with the poet's natural voice, the voice that he hears as the ideal speaker of the lines he is making up. I would like to digress slightly in order to illustrate what I mean more fully.

In his novel, *The First Circle*, Solzhenytzyn sets the action in a prison camp on the outskirts of Moscow where the inmates are all highly skilled technicians forced to labour at projects devised by Stalin. The most important of these is an attempt to devise a mechanism to bug a phone. But what is to be special about this particular bugging device is that it will not simply record the voice and the message but that it will identify the essential sound patterns of the speaker's voice, it will discover, in the words of the narrative, 'what it is that makes every human voice unique', so that no matter how he disguises his accent or changes his language, the fundamental structure of his voice will be caught. The idea was that a voice is like a fingerprint, possessing a constant and unique signature that can, like a fingerprint, be recorded and employed for identification.

Now one of the purposes of a literary education as I experienced it was to turn your ear into a poetic bugging device, so that a piece of verse denuded of name and date could be identified by its diction, tropes and cadences. And this secret policing of English verse was also based on the idea of a style as a signature. But what I wish to suggest is that there is a connection between the core of a poet's speaking voice and the core of his poetic voice, between his original accent and his discovered style. I think that the discovery of a way of writing that is natural and adequate to your sensibility depends on the recovery of that essential quick which Solzhenytzyn's technicians were trying to pin down. The quick is the absolute register to which proper poetic music has to be tuned.

How, then, do you find this voice? In practice, you hear it coming from somebody else, you hear something in another writer's sounds that flows in through your ear and enters the echo-chamber of your head and delights your whole nervous system in such a way that your reaction will be, 'Ah, I wish I had said that, in that particular way.' This other writer, in fact, has spoken something essential to you, something you recognize instinctively as a true sounding of aspects of yourself and your experience. And your first steps as a writer will be to imitate, consciously or unconsciously, those sounds that flowed in, that influence.

One of the writers who influenced me in this way was Gerard Manley Hopkins. The result of reading Hopkins at school was the desire to write, and when I first put pen to paper at university, what flowed out was what had flowed in, the bumpy alliterating music, the reporting sounds and richochetting consonants typical of Hopkins's verse. I remember lines from a piece I wrote called 'October Thought' in which some frail bucolic images foundered under the chainmail of the pastiche:

Starling thatch-watches, and sudden swallow
Straight breaks to mud-nest, home-rest rafter
Up past dry dust-drunk cobwebs, like laughter
Ghosting the roof of bog-oak, turf-sod and rods of willow . . .

and then there was 'heaven-hue, plum-blue and gorse-pricked with gold' and 'a trickling tinkle of bells well in the fold'.

Well, anyhow, looking back on that stuff by Hopkins out of Heaney, I believe there was a connection, not obvious at the time but, on reflection, real enough, between the heavily accented consonantal noise of Hopkins's poetic voice, and the peculiar regional characteristics of a Northern Ireland accent. The late W. R. Rodgers, another poet much lured by alliteration, said that the people from his (and my) part of the world were

                              an abrupt people
        Who like the spiky consonants of speech
        And think the soft ones cissy; who dig
        the k and t in orchestra, detect sin

> in sinfonia, get a kick out
> tin-cans, fricatives, fornication, staccato talk,
> anything that gives or takes attack
> like Micks, Teagues, tinker's gets, Vatican.

The Ulster accent is genrally a staccato consonantal one. Our tongue strikes the tangent of the consonant rather more than it rolls the circle of the vowel. It is energetic, angular, hard-edged, and it may be because of this affinity between my dialect and Hopkins's oddity that those first verses turned out as they did.

I couldn't say, of course, that I'd found a voice but I'd found a game. I knew the thing was only word-play, and I hadn't even the guts to put my name under it. I called myself *Incertus*, uncertain, a shy soul fretting and all that. I was in love with words themselves, had no sense of a poem as a whole structure and no experience of how the successful achievement of a poem could be a stepping stone in your life. Those verses were what one might call 'trial-pieces', little stiff inept designs in imitation of the master's fluent interlacing patterns, little heavy-handed clues by which the archaeologist can project the whole craft's mystery.

I was getting my first sense of crafting words and for one reason or another, words as bearers of history and mystery began to invite me. Maybe it had begun very early when my mother used to recite lists of affixes and suffixes, and Latin roots, with their English meanings, rhymes that formed part of her schooling in the early part of the century. Maybe it began with the exotic listing on the wireless dial: Stuttgart, Leipzig, Oslo, Hilversum. Maybe it was stirred by the beautiful sprung rhythms of the old BBC weather forecast: Dogger, Rockall, Malin, Shetland, Faroes, Finisterre; or with the gorgeous and inane phraseology of the catechism such as 'the solemnization of marriage within forbidden degrees of kindred'; or with the litany of the Blessed Virgin that was part of the enforced poetry in our household: 'Tower of Gold, Ark of the Covenant, Gate of Heaven, Morning Star, Health of the Sick, Refuge of Sinners, Comforter of the Afflicted.' None of these things were consciously savoured at the time but I think the fact that I still recall them with ease, and can delight in them as verbal music, means that they were bedding the foundation of my ear with a kind of linguistic hard-core that could be built on some day.

That was the unconscious bedding, but poetry involves a conscious centring on words also. This came by way of reading poetry itself, and being required to learn pieces by heart, phrases even, like Keats's, from *Lamia*:

> and his vessel now
> Grated the quaystone with her brazen prow,

or Wordsworth's

> All shod with steel,
> We hiss'd along the polished ice,

or Tennyson's:

> Old yew, which graspest at the stones
> That name the underlying dead,
> Thy fibres net the dreamless head,
> Thy roots are wrapped about the bones.

These were picked up in my last years at school, touchstones of sorts, where the language could give you a kind of aural goose-flesh. At the university I was delighted in the first weeks to meet the moody energies of John Webster—'I'll make Italian cutworks in their guts / If ever I return'—and later on to encounter the pointed masonry of Anglo-Saxon verse and to learn about the rich stratifications of the English language itself. Words alone were certain good. I even went so far as to write these 'Lines to myself':

> In poetry I wish you would
> Avoid the lilting platitude.
> Give us poems humped and strong,
> Laced tight with thongs of song,
> Poems that explode in silence
> Without forcing, without violence.
> Whose music is strong and clear and good
> Like a saw zooming in seasoned wood.
> You should attempt concrete expression,
> Half-guessing, half-expression.

Ah well. Behind that was 'Ars Poetica', Macleish's and Verlaine's, and Eliot's 'objective correlative' (half understood) and several critical essays (by myself and others) about 'concrete realization'. At the university, however, I kept the whole thing at arm's length, read poetry for the noise and wrote about half a dozen pieces for the literary magazine. But nothing happened inside me. No experience. No epiphany. All craft—and not much of that—and no technique.

I think technique is different from craft. Craft is what you can learn from other verse. Craft is the skill of making. It wins competitions in the *New Statesman*. It can be deployed without reference to the feelings or the self. It knows how to keep up a capable verbal athletic display; it can be content to be *vox et praeterea nihil*—all voice and nothing else, but not voice as in 'finding a voice'. Learning the craft is learning to turn the windlass at the well of poetry. Usually you begin by dropping the bucket half-way down the shaft and winding up a taking of air. You are miming the real thing until one day the chain draws unexpectedly tight and you have dipped into waters that will continue to entice you back. You'll have broken the skin on the pool of yourself. Your praties will be 'fit for digging'.

At that point it becomes appropriate to speak of technique rather than craft. Technique, as I would define it, involves not only a poet's way with words, his management of metre, rhythm and verbal texture; it involves also a definition of his stance towards life, a definition of his own reality. It involves the discovery of ways to go out of his normal cognitive bounds and raid the inarticulate: it entails the watermarking of your essential patterns of perception, voice and thought into the touch and texture of your lines; it is that whole creative effort of the mind's and body's resources to bring the meaning of experience within the jurisdiction of form. Technique is what turns, in Yeats's phrase, 'the bundle of accident and incoherence that sits down to breakfast' into 'an idea, something intended, complete'.

If I were asked for a figure who represents pure technique, I would say a water diviner. You can't learn the craft of dousing or divining—it's a gift for being in touch with what is there, hidden and real, a gift for mediating between the latent resource and the community that wants it current and released. If I might be permitted a sleight of quote, as it were, I would draw your attention to Sir Philip Sidney's animadversion in his *Apologie for Poetry*: 'Among the Romans a Poet was called *Vates*, which is as much as a Diviner . . .'

I once wrote a poem about this image. The diviner resembles the poet in his function of making contact with what lies hidden, and in his ability to make palpable what was sensed or raised.

The Diviner

Cut from the green hedge a forked hazel stick
That he held tight by the arms of the V:
Circling the terrain, hunting the pluck
Of water, nervous, but professionally

Unfussed. The pluck came sharp as a sting.
The rod jerked with precise convulsions,

> Spring water suddenly broadcasting
> Through a green hazel its secret stations.
>
> The bystanders would ask to have a try.
> He handed them the rod without a word.
> It lay dead in their grasp till nonchalantly
> He gripped expectant wrists. The hazel stirred.

What I had taken as matter of fact as a youngster became a matter of wonder in memory. I'm pleased when I look at the thing now that it ends with a verb, 'stirred', the heart of the mystery; and I'm also glad that 'stirred' chimes with 'word', bringing the two functions of Sir Philip Sidney's *vates* into the one sound.

I suppose technique is what allows that first stirring of the mind round a word or an image or a memory to grow towards articulation, articulation not necessarily in terms of argument or explication but in terms of its own potential for harmonious self-reproduction. The seminal excitement has to be granted conditions in which, in Hopkins's words, it 'selves, goes itself . . . crying What I do is me, for that I came'. Technique ensures that the first gleam attains its proper effulgence. Frost put it this way: 'a poem begins as a lump in the throat, a homesickness, a lovesickness. It finds the thought and the thought finds the words'. As far as I'm concerned, technique is more vitally and sensitively connected with that first activity where the 'lump in throat' finds 'the thought' than with 'the thought' finding 'the words'. That first epiphany involves the divining, vatic, oracular function; the second, the making, crafting function. To say, as Auden did, that a poem is a 'verbal contraption' is to keep one or two tricks up your sleeve.

Traditionally an oracle speaks in riddles, yielding its truths in disguise, offering its insights cunningly. And in the practice of poetry, there is a corresponding occasion of disguise, a protean, chameleon moment when the lump in the throat takes protective colouring in the new element of thought. One of the best documented occasions in the canon of English poetry, as far as this process is concerned, is a poem that survived in spite of its blemish. In fact, the blemish has earned it a peculiar fame:

> High on a mountain's highest ridge,
> Where oft the stormy winter gale
> Cuts like a scythe, while through the clouds
> It sweeps from vale to vale;

> Not five yards from the mountain path,
> This thorn you on your left espy;
> And to the left, three yards beyond,
> You see a little muddy pond
> Of water never dry;
> I've measured it from side to side:
> 'Tis three feet long and two feet wide.

That final couplet was probably more ridiculed than any other lines in *The Lyrical Ballads* yet Wordsworth maintained 'they ought to be liked'. That was in 1815, seventeen years after the poem had been composed; but five years later he changed the lines to 'Though but of compass small, and bare / To thirsting suns and parching air'. Craft, in more senses than one.

Yet far more important than the revision, for the purposes of this discussion, is Wordsworth's account of the poem's genesis. 'The Thorn', he wrote in a letter of 1843,

> arose out of my observing on the ridge of Quantock Hills, on a stormy day, a thorn which I had often passed in calm and bright weather without noticing it. I said to myself, 'Cannot I by some invention do as much to make this thorn permanently an impressive object, as the storm has made it to my eyes at this moment?' I began the poem accordingly, and composed it with great rapidity.

The storm, in other words, was nature's technique for granting the thorn its epiphany, awakening in Wordsworth that engendering, heightened state which he describes at the beginning of *The Prelude*—again in relation to the inspiring influence of wind:

> For I, methought, while the sweet breath of Heaven
> Was blowing on my body, felt within
> A corresponding, mild, creative breeze,
> A vital breeze which travell'd gently on
> O'er things which it had made, and is become
> A tempest, a redundant energy
> Vexing its own creation.

This is exactly the kind of mood in which he would have 'composed with great rapidity'; the measured recollection of the letter where he makes the poem sound as if it were written to the thesis propounded (retrospectively) in the revised *Preface*—'cannot I by some invention make this thorn permanently an impressive object?'—probably tones down an instinctive, instantaneous recognition into a rational procedure. The technical triumph was to discover a means of allowing his slightly abnormal, slightly numinous vision of the thorn to 'deal out its being'.

What he did to turn 'the bundle of accident and incoherence' of that moment into 'something intended, complete' was to find, again in Yeats's language, a mask. The poem as we have it is a ballad in which the speaker is a garrulous superstitious man, a sea captain, according to Wordsworth, who connects the thorn with murder and distress. For Wordsworth's own apprehension of the tree, he instinctively recognized, was basically superstitious: it was a standing over, a survival in his own sensibility of a magical way of responding to the natural world, of reading phenomena as signs, occurrences requiring divination. And in order to dramatize this, to transpose the awakened appetites in his consciousness into the satisfactions of a finished thing, he needed his 'objective correlative' which was, I suppose, what they called a mask in St Louis. To make the thorn 'permanently an impressive object', images and ideas from different parts of his conscious and unconscious mind were attracted by almost magnetic power. The thorn in its new, wind-tossed aspect had become a field of force.

Into this field were drawn memories of what the ballads call 'the cruel mother', who murders her own baby:

> She leaned her back against a thorn
> All around the loney-o
> And there her little babe was born
> Down by the greenwood side-o

is how a surviving version runs in Ireland. But there have always been variations on this pattern of the woman who kills her baby and buries it. And the ballads are also full of conclusions where briars and roses and thorns grow out of graves in symbolic token of the life and death of the buried one. So in Wordsworth's imagination the thorn grew into a symbol of tragic, feverish death, and to voice this the ballad mode came naturally; he donned the traditional mask of the tale-teller, legitimately credulous, entering and enacting a convention. The poem itself is a rapid and strange foray where Wordsworth discovered a way of turning the 'lump in the throat' into a 'thought', discovered a set of images, cadences and sounds that amplified his original visionary excitement into 'a redundant energy / Vexing its own creation':

> And some had sworn an oath that she
> Should be to public justice brought;
> And for the little infant's bones

With spades they would have sought.
But then the beauteous hill of moss
Before their eyes began to stir;
And for full fifty yards around
The grass it shook upon the ground.

I have spent this time on 'The Thorn' because it is a nicely documented example of feeling getting into words, in ways that parallel much in my own experience; although I must say that is hard to discriminate between feeling getting into words and words turning into feeling, and it is only on posthumous occasions that the distinction arises. Moreover, it is generally conceded that it may be dangerous for a writer to become too self-conscious about his own processes: to name them too definitively may have the effect of confining them to what is named. A poem always has elements of accident about it, which can be made the subject of inquest afterwards, but there is always a risk in conducting your own inquest. Robert Graves's 'Dance of Words' puts this delightfully:

To make them move, you should start from lightning
And not forecast the rhythm: rely on chance
Or so-called chance for its bright emergence
Once lightning interpenetrates the dance.

Grant them their own traditional steps and postures
But see they dance it out again and again
Until only lightning is left to puzzle over—
The choreography plain and the theme plain.

What we are engaged upon here is a way of seeing that turns the lightning into 'the visible discharge of electricity between cloud and cloud or between cloud and ground' rather than its own puzzling, brilliant self. There is nearly always an element of the bolt from the blue about a poem's origin.

When I called my second book of poems *Door into the Dark*, I intended to gesture towards this idea of poetry as a point of entry into the buried life of the feelings or as a point of exit for it. Words themselves are doors; Janus is to a certain extent their deity, looking back to a ramification of roots and associations and forward to a clarification of sense and meaning. And there are a number of poems that arise out of the almost unnameable energies that, for me, hovered over certain bits of language and landscape. The poem 'Undine' for example. It was the dark pool of the sound of the word that first took me: if our auditory imaginations were sufficiently attuned to plumb and sound a vowel, to

unite the most primitive and civilized associations, the word
'undine' would probably suffice as a poem in itself. *Unda*, a
wave, *undine*, a water-woman—a litany of undines would have ebb
and flow, water and woman, wave and tide, fulfilment and ex-
haustion in its very rhythms. But, old two-faced vocable that it is,
I discovered a more precise definition once, by accident, in a dictionary. An undine is a water-sprite who has to marry a human
being and have a child by him before she can become human.
With that definition, the lump in the throat, or rather the thump
in the ear, *undine*, became a thought, a field of force that called up
other images. One of these was an orphaned memory, without a
context, obviously a very early one, of watching a man clearing
out an old spongy growth from a drain between two fields, focus-
ing in particular on the way the water, in the cleared-out place, as
soon as the shovelfuls of sludge had been removed, the way the
water began to run free, rinse itself clean of the soluble mud and
make its own little channels and currents. And this image was
gathered into a more conscious reading of the myth as being
about the liberating, humanizing effect of sexual encounter.
Undine was a cold girl who got what the dictionary called a soul
through the experience of physical love. So the poem uttered
itself out of that nexus into the voice of the undine herself:

> He slashed the briars, shovelled up grey silt
> To give me right of way in my own drains
> And I ran quick for him, cleaned out my rust.
>
> He halted, saw me finally disrobed,
> Running clear, with apparent unconcern.
> Then he walked by me. I rippled and I churned
>
> Where ditches intersected near the river
> Until he dug a spade deep in my flank
> And took me to him. I swallowed his trench
>
> Gratefully, dispersing myself for love
> Down in his roots, climbing his brassy grain—
> But once he knew my welcome, I alone
>
> Could give him subtle increase and reflection.
> He explored me so completely, each limb
> Lost its cold freedom. Human, warmed to him.

When I read that poem once in a convent school, I said it was a
myth about agriculture, about the way water is tamed and hum-
anized when streams become irrigation canals, when water be-

comes involved with seed. And maybe that's as good an explanation as any. I like the para-phrasable extensions of a poem to be
as protean as possible, and yet I like its elements to be as firm as
possible. Words can allow you that two-faced approach also.
They stand smiling at the audience's way of reading them and
winking back at the poet's way of using them.

Behind this, of course, there is a good bit of symbolist theory.
Not that I am in any way consciously directed by symbolist pre-
scriptions in my approach to the composition of poems, but I am
sympathetic to a whole amalgam of commonplaces that might
vaguely deserve that label, from Rimbaud's notion of vowels as
colours and poetry as an alchemy of sounds to Yeats's notion of
the work of art as a 'masterful image'. And the stylistic tenets of
imagism as well as the aesthetics of symbolism I find attractive:
to present an image, 'an intellectual and emotional complex in a
moment of time'. I suppose all this was inevitable for me, given a
conventional course in English literature that culminated with
Eliot and Yeats.

In practice, however, you proceed by your own experience of
what it is to write what you consider a successful poem. You are
confirmed by the visitation of the last poem and threatened by
the elusiveness of the next one, and the best moments are those
when your mind seems to implode and words and images rush of
their own accord into the vortex. Which happened to me once
when the line 'We have no prairies' drifted into my head at bed-
time, and loosened a fall of images that constitute the poem
'Bogland'.

I had been vaguely wishing to write a poem about bogland,
chiefly because it is a landscape that has a strange assuaging effect
on me, one with associations reaching back into early childhood.
We used to hear about bog-butter, butter kept fresh for a great
number of years under the peat. Then when I was at school the
skeleton of an elk had been taken out of a bog nearby and a few of
our neighbours had got their photographs in the paper, peering
out across its antlers. So I began to get an idea of bog as the
memory of the landscape, or as a landscape that remembered
everything that happened in and to it. Moreover, since memory
was the faculty that supplied me with the first quickening of my
own poetry, I had a tentative unrealized need to make a congru-
ence between memory and bogland and, for the want of a better
word, our national consciousness. And it all released itself after
'We have no prairies . . .'—but we have bogs.

At that time I was teaching modern literature in Queen's Uni-

versity, Belfast, and had been reading about the frontier and the
west as an important myth in the American consciousness, so I
set up—or rather, laid down—the bog as an answering Irish myth. I
wrote it quickly the next morning, having slept on my excitement, and revised it on the hoof, from line to line:

> We have no prairies
> To slice a big sun at evening—
> Everywhere the eye concedes to
> Encroaching horizon,
>
> Is wooed into the cyclops' eye
> Of a tarn. Our unfenced country
> Is bog that keeps crusting
> Between the sights of the sun.
>
> They've taken the skeleton
> Of the Great Irish Elk
> Out of the peat, set it up
> An astounding crate full of air.
>
> Butter sunk under
> More than a hundred years
> Was recovered salty and white.
> The ground itself is kind, black butter
>
> Melting and opening underfoot,
> Missing its last definition
> By millions of years.
> They'll never dig coal here,
>
> Only the waterlogged trunks
> Of great firs, soft as pulp.
> Our pioneers keep striking
> Inwards and downwards,
>
> Every layer they strip
> Seems camped on before.
> The bogholes might be Atlantic seepage.
> The wet centre is bottomless.

Again, as in the case of 'Digging', the seminal impulse had been
unconscious. I believe what generated the poem about memory
was something lying beneath the very floor of memory, something I only connected with the poem months after it was written,
which was a warning that older people would give us about going
into the bog. They were afraid we might fall into the pools in the
old workings, so they put it about (and we believed them) that

there was no bottom in the bogholes. Little did they—or I—know that I would filch it for the last line of a book.

There was also in that book a poem called 'Requiem for the Croppies', which was written in 1966 when most poets in Ireland were straining to celebrate the anniversary of the 1916 Rising. Typically, I suppose, I went further back. 1916 was the harvest of seeds sown in 1798, when revolutionary republican ideals and national feeling coalesced in the doctrines of Irish republicanism and in the rebellion of 1798 itself—unsuccessful and savagely put down. The poem was born of and ended with an image of resurrection based on the fact that, some time after the rebels were buried in common graves, these graves began to sprout with young barley, growing up from barley corn the insurgent forces, or 'croppies', had carried in their pockets to eat while on the march. The oblique implication was that the seeds of violent resistance sowed in the Year of Liberty had flowered in what Yeats called 'the right rose tree' of 1916. I did not realize at the time that the original heraldic murderous encounter between Protestant yeoman and Catholic rebel was to be initiated again in the summer of 1969, in Belfast, two months after the book was published.

From that moment the problems of poetry moved from being simply a matter of achieving the satisfactory verbal icon to being a search for images and symbols adequate to our predicament. I do not mean liberal lamentation that citizens should feel compelled to murder one another or deploy their different military arms over the matter of nomenclatures such as British or Irish. I do not mean public celebrations or execrations of resistance or atrocity—although there is nothing necessarily unpoetic about such celebration, if one thinks of 'Easter 1916'. I mean that I felt it imperative to discover a field of force in which, without abandoning fidelity to the processes and experience of poetry as I have outlined them, it would be possible to encompass the perspectives of a humane reason and at the same time to grant the religious intensity of the violence its deplorable authenticity and complexity. And when I say religious, I am not thinking simply of the sectarian division. To some extent the enmity can be viewed as a struggle between the cults and devotees of a god and a goddess. There is an indigenous territorial numen, a tutelar of the whole island, call her Mother Ireland, Kathleen Ni Houlihan, the poor old woman, the Shan Van Vocht, whatever; and her sovereignty has been temporarily usurped or infringed by a new male cult whose founding fathers were Cromwell, William of Orange and

Edward Carson, and whose godhead is incarnate in a rex or caesar resident in a palace in London. What we have is the tail-end of a struggle in a province between territorial piety and imperial power.

Now I realize that this idiom is remote from the agnostic world of economic interest whose iron hand operates in the velvet glove of 'talks between elected representatives', and remote from the political manoeuvres of power-sharing; but it is not remote from the psychology of the Irishmen and Ulstermen who do the killing, and not remote from the bankrupt psychology and mythologies implicit in the terms Irish Catholic and Ulster Protestant. The question, as ever, is 'How with this rage shall beauty hold a plea?' And my answer is, by offering 'befitting emblems of adversity'.

Some of those emblems I found in a book that was published, appositely, in the year the killing started, 1969. And again appositely, it was entitled *The Bog People*. It was chiefly concerned with preserved bodies of men and women found in the bogs of Jutland, naked, strangled or with their throats cut, disposed under the peat since early Iron Age times. The author, P. V. Glob, argues convincingly that a number of these, and in particular, the Tollund Man, whose head is now preserved near Aarhus in the museum at Silkeburg, were ritual sacrifices to the Mother Goddess, the goddess of the ground who needed new bridegrooms each winter to bed with her in her sacred place, in the bog, to ensure the renewal and fertility of the territory in the spring. Taken in relation to the tradition of Irish political martyrdom for the cause whose icon is Kathleen Ni Houlihan, this is more than an archaic barbarous rite: it is an archetypal pattern. And the unforgettable photographs of these victims blended in my mind with photographs of atrocities, past and present, in the long rites of Irish political and religious struggles. When I wrote this poem, I had a completely new sensation, one of fear. It is a vow to go on pilgrimage and I felt as it came to me—and again it came quickly—that unless I was deeply in earnest about what I was saying, I was simply invoking dangers for myself. It is called 'The Tollund Man':

I

Some day I will go to Aarhus
To see his peat-brown head,
The mild pods of his eye-lids,
His pointed skin cap.

In the flat country nearby
Where they dug him out,
His last gruel of winter seeds
Caked in his stomach,

Naked except for
The cap, noose and girdle,
I will stand a long time.
Bridegroom to the goddess,

She tightened her torc on him
And opened her fen,
Those dark juices working
Him to a saint's kept body,

Trove of the turfcutters'
Honeycombed workings.
Now his stained face
Reposes at Aarhus.

II
I could risk blasphemy,
Consecrate the cauldron bog
Our holy ground and pray
Him to make germinate

The scattered, ambushed
Flesh of labourers,
Stockinged corpses
Laid out in the farmyards,

Tell-tale skin and teeth
Flecking the sleepers
Of four young brothers, trailed
For miles along the lines.

III
Something of his sad freedom
As he rode the tumbril
Should come to me, driving,
Saying the names

Tollund, Grauballe, Nebelgard,
Watching the pointing hands
Of country people,
Not knowing their tongue.

Out there in Jutland
In the old man-killing parishes
I will feel lost,
Unhappy and at home.

Just how persistent the barbaric attitudes are not only in the slaughter but in the psyche I discovered, again when the frisson of the poem itself had passed, and indeed after I had fulfilled the vow and gone to Jutland, 'the holy blisful martyr for to seke'. I read the following in a chapter on 'The Religion of the Pagan Celts' by the Celtic scholar, Anne Ross:

> Moving from sanctuaries and shrines . . . we come now to consider the nature of the actual deities . . . But before going on to look at the nature of some of the individual deities and their cults, one can perhaps bridge the gap, as it were by considering a symbol which, in its way, sums up the whole of Celtic pagan religion and is as representative of it as is, for example, the sign of the cross in Christian contexts. This is the symbol of the severed human head; in all its various modes of iconographic representation and verbal presentation, one may find the hard core of Celtic religion. It is indeed . . . a kind of shorthand symbol for the entire religious outlook of the pagan Celts.

My sense of occasion and almost awe as I vowed to go to pray to the Tollund Man and assist at his enshrined head had a longer ancestry than I had at the time realized.

I began by suggesting that my point of view involved poetry as divination, as a restoration of the culture to itself. In Ireland in this century it has involved for Yeats and many others an attempt to define and interpret the present by bringing it into significant relationship with the past, and I believe that that effort in our present circumstances has to be urgently renewed. But here we stray from the realm of technique into the realm of tradition; to forge a poem is one thing, to forge the uncreated conscience of the race, as Stephen Dedalus put it, is quite another and places daunting pressures and responsibilities on anyone who would risk the name of poet.

THE NOVELIST AS VICTIM

THOMAS HINDE, FRSL

Read 14 November 1974:
V. S. Pritchett, CBE, D Litt, FRSL, in the Chair

NEVER apologize, never explain, someone, I think E. M. Forster, said. Well, taking half his advice, I won't apologize for my talk this evening being almost exclusively autobiographical, because that was my brief, though I should warn you that its literary comparisons and learned allusions may give somewhat the appearance of having been dragged in by the scruffs of their necks. But as for explanation, here I must totally disregard him, for what I'm going to try to do consists entirely of explanation: explain how I feel as author about three of my own novels. How I felt when I invented them, as I wrote them, and perhaps, but to a much smaller extent, how I feel about them now—because the fact is—and I sometimes wonder how many writers are like me in this— that unless some chance like this evening's talk forces me, I never think about them. To return to Forster, as I shall again, I find the picture he once gave of himself in late middle age, gently turning over and re-reading his own novels, admiring what he had done well and regretting what he had done not so well, entirely foreign to my own inclination or habit.

Before launching into this orgy of explanation and confession, I should make one point, however obvious. I am not attempting and never would attempt to explain what these novels *are*. What I felt or feel about them, and what I meant them to be are quite irrelevant to them as they now exist. Even without questioning the whole basis of a common assessment of works of art, on the grounds that no two views of it can ever be the same, or going as far as Robbe-Grillet goes if I remember rightly and suggesting that every reader creates his own novel from the succession of provocative but in no sense definitive words he finds on the printed page, I do say with complete assurance that the least typical view of all will be the author's. He has brought to it all manner of hopes and intentions, whole areas of background image and association, which no reader can ever or indeed ever needs to know about. He is in every way the person least qualified to make an independent judgment of the book itself as it has finally been printed.

I must also warn you that your kind invitation to speak in a series of talks by experimental writers, or writers who have 'extended the frontiers of the form in which they work' as it was put to me, came as something of a surprise, because this is not on the whole the way in which I think of my own work. I have never for example tried or wanted to write in anything other than a quite simple style, communicating with normal words used in fairly normal syntax and grammar, the ideas and events of my stories. Though I admire Joyce, I have felt no inclination to imitate or advance beyond—if that were conceivable—his attempt to illustrate the actual word-working of the human mind in a kind of prose poem. The dictionary English of Nabokov or the purple passages of Laurence Durrell—so purple one sometimes suspects self-mockery—I find even less sympathetic.

But on second thoughts I do admit that my attempts to be a straightforward realistic novelist have been fairly regularly sabotaged by other urges, which may not have been stylistic but have led me to work just a little outside the stricter confines of realism both in content and structure. So it is the inventing and writing of these and the experiences from which they spring that I am going to describe. And this brings me at once to a very simple division between two basic impulses which I suggest drive the novelist—perhaps a writer in any medium—to his own particular style, form and content.

The first of these is the most obvious. The world impinges on him and he has things which he feels or thinks about it which demand expression. They go round and round inside his head, compelling him to search for the best words in which to express them so that he may then show them to as many people as possible—and as a result feel a little better. All people must have this urge to some degree, but I suspect that the writer is distinctive in that he is *less* capable of coping with real life, coming to terms with it, defending himself against it, whatever phrase you like to use, than most other people. He is a professional opter-out. At his best he is an idealist, who cannot bear the compromises of, say, politics, or merely of conversations in which he attempts to agree *exactly* with any single person about one single thing. Less flatteringly, he is a person who is too timid or ineffectual to take part in the real world, too unwilling to risk defeat by it perhaps, and retreats into a safer world of which he is the master. When Tolstoy said about his brother that he had all a writer's good qualities but none of the equally necessary bad ones, I suspect—though I have no historical evidence—that this was one of the things he was talking about. It was surely Tolstoy's own problem, and he himself was continually attempting to escape from the confines of desk and pen into real action, where he could be a man and not, as he saw it, a cowardly scribbler.

This as I say is the simple straightforward source of a writer's inspiration and the explanation of the nature of his work. But beside this I believe there also exists all the time in his mind quite a different kind of inspiration, concerned less with content than form. On the one hand this may be negative. If he is a novelist he may be in despair at the prospect of writing a novel in the realistic style and form which has been so thoroughly and successfully exploited over the past 200 years. And unless he is obsessed by the importance of the things he wishes to say, unless these need so powerfully to burst from him that he doesn't care much about the form they will take, this may be a very powerfully inhibiting thought. Lawrence, I suppose, is a writer who cared very little about originality of style or form, because he believed that what he had to say was important enough to transcend such trivial constrictions.

But most modern novelists do not have this sort of confidence, and as a result they are often forming in their minds vague ideas about the *sort of novel* they want to write, ideas not about their plots or characters, or even about the societies they live in, but about the kind of words in which they would like to communicate or the shape of some ideal book, attached at first to no particular person or story at all. They may for example get the idea of writing a novel in newspaper format, not to be read from cover to cover, but to be browsed in, as a newspaper is browsed in. Or of having holes in their pages for suggesting subliminally to readers ahead of time thoughts which they would normally only reach a chapter later. My own first steps along this path, the path of conceiving a book's form before its content, were a great deal less ambitious. I merely thought that I would like to write a spy story.

The theoretical justification for this was simple. The novel should entertain, I believed, and its form could be used to provide this entertainment, this heightening of the drama of life. Behind or inside the entertaining form I would be able to say the things I wanted to say about human nature and the world around me—or rather they would with luck emerge for at this point I certainly had no conceptualized ideas which I wanted to include. My models, too, were obvious: the works of Simenon, Chandler, Hamnet. Most of all Graham Greene's entertainments. All seemed to have succeeded in just this way.

But soon—almost instantly in fact—something went wrong. It became clear to me that I knew absolutely nothing about the world of spies and cops or their methods of operation. I had never met a spy, nor talked intimately with a policeman. Two alternatives presented themselves. Either I must do some conscientious research—something which at that time I was unwilling to do because I did not believe, however conscientious I might be, that I would ever get it exactly right. Or—here quite accidentally came the element which gives the book whatever originality it has— I must make the spy write in the first person and leave it uncertain whether or not he really is a spy. Because if I did this it didn't matter if he went a bit wrong about false heels or dead letter boxes. Later psychologists have assured me that the book which resulted from this quite technical idea—and was named *The Day the Call Came*—might have been the case history of a schizophrenic, but I can assure you that this wasn't my plan, and that at that time I wasn't even sure what were a schizophrenic's symptoms and had certainly never consciously observed one. I leave you to make the obvious and not entirely complimentary deduction about the author's state of mental health. As Jung is once reported to have said 'Bring me a man who is normal and I will cure him.'

It is certainly true that the private world of my spy, in which he receives messages, possibly or possibly not sent by himself, enters and searches his neighbours' houses and continually tries to detect which are friend and which foe, finally comes into a conflict which even he can't ignore with the world of the gin-drinking outer suburb in which he lives. The result, typical I'm told of a schizophrenic's syndrome, is blood and murder. Whether or not this spy story, perhaps all spy stories, are allegories of the artist's life I leave readers to decide—it certainly wasn't my conscious plan. Once more to give my opinion would be to attempt to tell you what the book *is*, something I'm least well qualified to do, as opposed to how it was made and what I wanted it to be. Though I must admit that a writer—or at least this one—does feel comfortable when impersonating a spy. It *is*, after all, his life-long role.

To discuss the next book intelligibly I must give you a little more personal background. I had gone to the Middle West to teach at one of those vast State universities—this one had 30,000 students and—somehow an even more daunting idea—3,000 faculty. It was my first visit to America, and also my first job, if that's the right word, for about five years during which I had only been a writer. It was also, incidentally, the sort of experience which has only been available to English writers since the last war. Dickens, Wilde, Kingsley and all those others who crossed the Atlantic in earlier times went as visiting celebrities to lecture, not to teach—very different things.

Once again I felt what I often experience in a new country or situation; an initial reluctance ever to use as material something so complex and diffuse, which I understood so little, followed after many months by the gradual build up of a compulsion to do exactly this. In an American university there was an additional complication: I was all too well aware that there were already many campus novels, a high proportion of them written by visiting British novelists. And even though I had taken the precaution of reading none of these, I had made a conscious decision that I wasn't going to add another.

What was to be the solution? To explain it I must refer again to what I have described as the novelist's second sort of inspiration, that which concerns not what he will put into his book, but the *sort of book* it will be, and refer you to the passage you must know in E. M. Forster's *Aspects of the Novel* in which he discusses Gide's *Les Faux Monnayeurs*, suggesting that it is a kind of grand extension of the novel, quite different from but of a parallel and equally exciting sort to Joyce's *Ulysses*: the novelist writing about a novelist as he writes his novel, with this novel printed alongside the diary the fictional novelist keeps while writing it. 'Gide has also published the diary he kept which he was writing *Les Faux Monnayeurs*,' Forster says, 'and there is no reason why he should not publish in future the impressions he had when rereading both the diary and the novel, and in the future-perfect a still more final synthesis in which the diary, the novel and his impressions of both will interact.'

I must also remind you of the passage in Isherwood's *Lions and Shadows* in which he discusses this part of Forster's book and how he and his friend Chalmers each read *Les Faux Monnayeurs*:

'The plot of this novel,' Isherwood writes, 'as described so thrillingly, suggestively and misleadingly, by E. M. Forster in his *Aspects*, excited our imagination beyond all bounds; indeed, the novel itself came as something of an anti-climax. In our impatience, we both bought copies and began reading simultaneously. We even reported our progress to each other on a series of postcards. Chalmers wrote: "Have just finished Chapter seven. The idiot has ruined everything." But later: "Page 359. Gide is the greatest. Whatever he does he can't spoil it now." What our final verdict was I forget. In fact, I have almost entirely forgotten what *Les Faux Monnayeurs* was actually about. What remains, immense, vague, profoundly exciting, is my conception of Forster's conception of Gide's original idea. One day I shall attempt the nearly hopeless task of fixing it and writing it down.'

Isherwood here describes exactly my own feelings both about Forster's description of *Les Faux Monnayeurs* and about my mild disappointment with the book itself. What remained with me was a vague but hopeless ambition, not so much to capture and describe Forster's description, as to discover some way of my own to carry forward and if possible cap this extension of the form of the novel.

And in retrospect I realize that when I solved to my own satisfaction the conflict between my pressing American material and my determination not to use it in the way it had been used all too often, this same ambition was still lurking in the background of my mind. What I suddenly saw that I might do was, instead of carefully avoid the visiting-British-lecturer's-campus-novel syndrome, to embrace it fully and totally. I would write what amounted to a parody of such books. Not only would I write about an American campus as seen by an innocent visiting British lecturer, but the hero of my novel, of course a visiting British lecturer, would also be writing a novel. And, needless to say, the subject of his novel would be an innocent visiting British lecturer on an American campus. Who, needless to say, would be writing a novel—but here comes the twist, his hero, the hero of the novel my fictional hero was writing, would be writing a novel of which *my* hero was the hero.

The result was not a plot of receding-mirror type, with endless innocent visisting British lecturers stretching smaller and smaller into the distance, but a circular one. Each was writing about someone who was writing about the other. Furthermore I left it in doubt—although I have my own view on the matter—which of them was 'real' and had in fact invented the other. They were to be called Maurice Peterson and Peter Morrison.

This was of course the merest framework for the novel, but it was a frame into which I could try to fit all those other ideas and new impressions which America in general and a Middle West campus in particular were giving me. And the first of these, the astonishing self-analysing quality of all Americans, allowed me to extend and I hope enhance the parody, because there are a number of other subsidiary characters in the book who are also writing books about each other. And this incidentally is the kind of sifting test through which I find myself putting any idea or episode, or indeed paragraph or sentence in a book: that it shall have not just one but at least two funtions. To take some very simple example, the words used to make a character cross a room, shall not only get him there, but also add some new element to his character, *and* perhaps manage by their tone to convey the time of day, the weather outside or the general drama or lack of drama of the occasion.

Then there was the university itself with all those likeable, keen but rather naïve students, who might innocently and sincerely come up to you after an exam you had set them and say, as one did to me, 'Gee sir, that was a real fine question, question three, I really had a ball answering that.' Imagine the inhibiting shame which an English student would suffer just at the idea of doing such a thing, the fear that because you couldn't fail to hear such flattery as sarcastic you would mark him lower for it, or that even if by any chance you heard it as sincere, you would mark him still lower for insulting you by such a crude attempt to influence you.

And of course there was the faculty itself, all those three thousand rather humourless but high-powered brains shut up together in that isolated township a hundred and fifty miles out on the prairie.

Still more pressing, there was the American female, in her student shape no less, in fact perhaps more self-concerned, self-analysing, worried and discontented. She indeed was the central problem of my two characters. Each had a girl—Gilda and Olga respectively, and each made his fictional self treat this girl in the sort of way he himself consciously or unconsciously longed to treat his own girl. Thus Peterson is deeply and romantically in love with Gilda. He writes about Morrison who treats Olga with a

gay and off-hand lustfulness, laying her here there and everywhere, eventually carrying her off to a thinly disguised New
Orleans. It is here that he, Morrison, makes an appalling discovery: he is actually falling in love with her. He also—the two
occur in parallel and are presumably related—discovers that she has
been being steadily unfaithful to him. Left as it seems to him
with no other choice, he disposes of her in the Mississippi and
settles down to write the novel he has been planning the whole
book but which till now he has not been able to begin, having at
last discovered its subject. And his first words, which conclude
my book, have also been the first words of mine, describing
Peterson writing about his own, Morrison's, funeral.

One further element of my American experience remained to
be included. For convenience I have extracted it and left it till
last, but in fact it was there from early on, and all emerged in
parallel and in a far less tidy way than I'm suggesting. This was
the American drug scene, then in its early and most appealing
flower-folk phase.

It is a hard subject to talk about. To some it will be old hat, to
others still criminal and reprehensible. Astonishing passions are
raised, and I realize that I shall raise some of them right away by
suggesting that these can be seen as a parallel to the passions
which were aroused in the last century by alcohol, alcoholism,
and teetotalism—at a time incidentally when opium was still easily
available from the chemist. So let me try to calm them by assur-
ing you that I am making no judgment on the social dangers or
benefits of drugs. Maybe we should have better societies if we all
smoked nothing and ate only nuts and vegetables—or maybe, as my
friends suggested at the time, there would be instant world peace
if Khruschev and Johnson would only go on a trip together. Instead I shall confine myself to my own experiences and these only
as far as they affected my writing.

They were by a long way the most interesting and exciting that
I had had for twenty years, perhaps ever. At the risk of oversim-
plification I want to divide them into two, suggesting an import-
ant contrast between two drug types, the one represented by
L.S.D. or Acid and the other by the amphetamines, specifically
Methadryn or Speed.

I'll pass quickly over many of the well known and by now quite
often described effects of Acid, the three-dimensional quality it
gives to pictures, the beautiful tiled caves you see if you close
your eyes and listen to music, the way you discover your teeth
again, a strange and marvellously succulent experience, the way

writing or any artistic expression suddenly seems an almost worthless, because hopeless, attempt at *translation*, since it can never begin to match the wonder of the actual experience . . . and concentrate instead on the one or two which were particularly relevant to my novel. The first of these, and in some ways central to the rest, was the way I returned to a childish fascination with *any* sight or sound or taste or even thought which impinged on my senses or mind and would only with great reluctance break off and attend to another. For instance I remember trying to make a telephone call. It was almost impossible, not because I couldn't physically do it but because the sight of my finger-tip in the dialling hole was so fascinating that all I wanted to do was go on staring at it. Someone once gave me the best answer to the question one is often asked about such trips: how incapable does it make one? 'Would you,' he said, 'send a three-year-old child to post a letter?' 'You wouldn't, not because he was physically incapable of doing it but because he would be so distracted and fascinated by the sights and sounds he met on the way that he would never reach the post box.'

Stemming at least partly from this acute and fascinated observation of everything you meet comes the other effect I want to describe: an acute sensitivity to the feelings of everyone you see or with whom you are tripping. Watching every tiny gesture they make, every tiny movement of their faces you see right into them and know exactly who they are and what their problems are. As a result you realize the utter absurdity of your paranoid anxieties about them. How can you be afraid of their dislike and hostility when it is clear that every one of them suffers just the same anxiety about what you are thinking about them? From this comes the most enormous sense of freedom, a kind of sloughing off of shame as something senseless, needless, almost incredible.

The character in my novel who takes Acid is Peterson, the ineffectual romantic one, and perhaps I could quote a passage here to give an idea of the place it plays in the whole novel and just why the novel has its title: *High*.

> 'Think about my story' [Peterson writes] 'and see if new ideas come.' Nothing comes.
>
> Presently, on a fresh sheet he writes, 'Still thinking about whether I should be making these notes.'
>
> On a third sheet he writes, 'Thinking about thinking, about thinking (about thinking?) . . .' And later. 'Back to base one—wondering why I'm doing this and if I should be. Pen has rainbow point.'

On another sheet he begins, 'Back to that story,' and presently, 'No better. Mind won't take hold of it.'

Unexpectedly the second sheet now reappears where he reads, 'Still thinking about whether I should be . . .' Something clicks in his mind. An idea. He knows, too, on which sheet he should write it—the third—but he can't find it. The sheets begin to get badly muddled. He gets some on to his lap. He gets some back on to the settee. Now some are on his left as well as on his right.

'Having fun?' Jill says.

Indeed he is having fun. At the same time that he's anxious to find the sheet to which to add his first useful idea, he's deliciously amused by his own inefficiency, by the chaos, near snowstorm proportions, of the papers he's turning, shuffling, inverting, and letting slip to the floor. Arbitrarily he choses a blank sheet and writes.

'Idea: each time you reread a sentence—about an experience—it's a new experience. So writing becomes the constant revising of one basic descriptive sentence.'

Nothing follows for a long time. Perhaps nothing can. 'Preoccupied with why I so enjoyed that private party with my papers,' he writes.

He stares at his two sandals, which he's put on the table, among the ashtrays and dirty cheeseburger plates. He writes, *'Who is Morrison writing about?'* He knows he must underline this because it's central, but he's forgotten why it's central. Instead, he becomes preoccupied with his two sandals. There they are on the table. They are Maurice Peterson and Peter Morrison. The incredible appropriateness of this astounds him. He crosses his feet. Now Maurice Peterson and Peter Morrison have changed places. It leaves him aghast. He *knows* it's significant, but just why is tantalizingly beyond his grasp. He strains and strains to reach it, but at the moment when he almost has it, he becomes unsure whether or not it *is* significant.

He collects the sheets he has written on, and a lot of blank ones he can't separate, folds them and puts them in an inside pocket of his jacket. The significance of that! With the power of a revelation he sees that he has spent his whole life folding up little sheets of paper and putting them in an inside pocket. In a single act he has summed up his character. Jill is watching him. She has understood too.

The unnecessariness of it appals him. He wants to take them

out and spread them about. Look at them, see what's written
on them. If you laugh it's because of your own anxious de-
fensive lives. Now he knows how he can live in future. He has
gripped the message life has been offering him, for months,
perhaps ever since he came to this country.

Ideas race in his mind. Every idea is greater *in* itself for
being greater *than* itself. And greatest of all is the solution to
this, his greatest, everyone's greatest problem. How to live without shame. To learn it he has had to make this trip, THIS
AMERICAN TRIP—he no longer knows which he is thinking
about. He can no longer distinguish the difference. He no
longer believes there is any difference . . .

In my opinion the real theme of the novel, *High*, emerged
as my own, and indeed every Englishman's, great American
trip.

But inside this Acid trip there is another: whereas the cry of
the Acid head is 'Wow, oh wow,' meaning, Just look at that, isn't
it the most *wonderful, significant, symbolic* thing you ever saw, how
can you begin to try to *describe* it—so the cry of the taker of methadryn or speed freak as he was called is, 'Go go.'

He experiences effects the exact opposite of those I've been
describing. Far from wanting to sit and watch he wants to do and
think. His feet itch to move him, anywhere, but fast. His molars
set and grind (speed freaks have actually broken their own teeth)
and his mind is filled with astonishing conceptualizing energy.
Every thought that comes into it he wants to categorize, expand
in a dozen different ways, play experimental thought games with.
If you'll excuse one further quotation perhaps it will explain what
I mean: Morrison the lustful one is phoning home to his wife to
say that he has gone off to New Orleans without telling her.

'I've been called away, dear. Urgent. A possible film con-
tract . . .'
'Your pyjamas . . .' she began.
Pyjamas historical, pyjamas racial, pyjamas social, classes
who wore them, age groups who didn't. Pyjamas philological—
what a word—pyjamas erotic—nylon, rubber, corduroy. The
astonishing habit of taking off one lot of clothes to go to bed
in another, the fact, as clear as any of these, that she'd ceased to
think about his pyjamas before she'd said the word, that they'd
emerged as a meaningless exclamation, a sort of gasp of fright.
Each of these possible directions for pyjamas to lead him came
at the same instant, each fascinated him. Holding them all in

his mind, he could choose from them as if they were labelled drawers in a chest, knew that while explaining the contents of one he could hold in his mind the knowledge of all the others and of where this one fitted into the total pyjama pattern . . .

Just as it seemed to me appropriate for Peterson to take the acid trip, so his creation (and/or creator) Morrison takes the speed trip. Indeed during the whole of the final section of the book, Morrison's visit to the south, where he utimately discovers his love for Olga and destroys her, they are both speeding.

Well I hope that this gives you some idea of the processes which led to what must I suppose at least in its shape be called an experimental novel—perhaps also in its attempt to cope with new subject-matter, because although such writers as de Quincey and Coleridge wrote under the influence of opium, acid and speed were at that time newish experiences. Though I have, as I say, made these processes seem a lot tidier and more logical than in fact they were. As Tolstoy again said, 'No writer ever finishes a book, he only abandons it,' and if I have had this feeling about most of my books I have had it most strongly about *High*.

I'd like now to turn to the third of my books I'm going to talk about, one of quite a different sort, though the setting and inspiration were again American.

In discussing the effects of America I have intentionally left till now those which, as a writer, I experienced when I attempted to become an academic and teach in an academic way classes about the English (or British, as we had to call it) novel. These were in almost every way highly disturbing. For example, I can honestly say that the first literature class I ever attended was one for graduate students which I was myself meant to be conducting.

But as time passed I grew both cunning and indeed fascinated by the new and alien attitude to novels which these classes and my students demanded.

I learnt what was meant by the New Criticism—something I'd been totally ignorant about before—and many subsequent if more ephemeral schools. I read Northrop Frye, and, still more influential, such current campus best-sellers as Joseph Cambell's *Hero with a Thousand Faces* and Eric Neuman's *History of Consciousness*, all books which—to oversimplify—attempts to show underlying Jungian patterns in art and literature. More generally, I found it impossible to retain my earlier innocence about the techniques, symbols, mythic content and many other features of novels, including any I might now write myself, and I realized

that unless I regained it—something which at the time seemed im-
probable—I should be for ever in a state of mind in which I was
analysing my writing as soon as if not before I was synthesizing
it.

My idea of the *sort of book* I wanted to write also changed. How
could I bear ever again merely to create a traditional straightforward novel of realistic events, narrative and dialogue—which as my
teaching had shown me, might exhaust all there was to be said
about it in a single class session, when it had been time-tabled to
occupy three?

As a result I was faced with another and similar problem. The
solution was not the same but perhaps parallel. Instead of shying
away from this consciously self-analysed and artificially construc-
ted novel I would as it were take the bull by the horns and write
one which amounted to a *reductio ad absurdum* of the genre.

Once again the real world impinged on this theoretical concept,
or rather I selected from the world around me the elements which
would fit it. First of these was Boston's at that time only high-rise
block, the Prudential Building. Suddenly, looking at it in the new
way I've described, I saw how perfectly it symbolized the
country's worship of materialism and was indeed almost a replica
of the cathedrals of the religions of other societies. First there was
this gigantic central tower block—the cathedral's tower or spire.
Then there were the shopping arcades which clustered around its
feet—its many little side chapels. How appropriate that the shops in
these arcades, their windows filled with beautiful goods at enormous prices, did little real business. People came there to gaze with
wonder, close to worship, at English tweed suits and Chinese
ivory chess sets before hurrying off to suburban discount base-
ments to buy inferior replicas at a quarter the price.

At this point another artificial influence intruded. I was teaching Conrad's *Under Western Eyes*, and seeing how perfectly its plot
fitted an analysis of the Jungian sort which the writers I've mentioned, Joseph Campbell, and in particular Eric Neuman suggested, almost more perfectly than *Heart of Darkness* which is the
archetypal book for this sort of critical treatment. In brief,
Conrad's hero makes not just one but two journeys through the
underword before destroying his dragon mother in a scene which
is more redolent of sexual fulfilment and death than any I know,
while superficially retaining a Victorian propriety, before becoming reconciled with his heavenly father and thus obtaining his
release.

From Conrad came the idea of a student traitor, and from the

real world of the campus came the current form it took: that my
hero, Jo, a clean upright country boy, should be invited to do
something which his mind approved of but his instincts recoiled
from: become a C.I.A. spy on his fellow students. This was to be
Jo's journey through the underworld.

The conclusion was missing and so too was the queen goddess.
Just how I came to these I have forgotten, but I know that a
phrase in Northrop Frye's *Anatomy of Criticism*, played a part.
Somewhere he writes—about some book which he is analysing—
that its subject is of course human sacrifice. In my innocence it
seemed to me that I would rather like to write a story which had
this concealed subject. I took the inevitable next step, went to *The
Golden Bough* and looked in the index for references to Sacrifice,
human.

There are surprisingly few—four or five as far as I can remember—
but gradually I saw how perfectly the most complete of these
suited my purpose.

'A certain country is infested with a many-headed serpent,
dragon or other monster, which would destroy the whole people
if a human victim, generally a virgin, were not delivered up to
him periodically. Many of the victims have perished, and at last it
has fallen to the lot of the king's own daughter to be sacrificed.
She is exposed to the monster, but the hero of the tale, generally
a young man of humble birth, interposes in her behalf, slays the
monster and receives the hand of the princess as his reward. In
many tales the monster, who is some times described as a serpent,
inhabits the water of a sea, a lake or a fountain. In other versions
he is a serpent or dragon . . .'

This passage plays two parts in the book. It forms part of the
reading for one of Jo's courses. Needless to say he is studying
World Religions. And it is the story of the whole book. Sherry,
the heroine, who has been her high school queen, is the sacrifice.
She becomes involved with the twin monsters haunting America,
drug-taking monsters and anarchist monsters. Nic, a hippy who
stands for the first of these, wears a gigantic silver snake on his
forearm and Jo first meets him when he entices Sherry far out to
sea and almost drowns her. Jo is the young man of humble birth,
and his journey through the underworld is made to rescue Sherry
from the appalling friends to which society has exposed her as its
sacrifice. The climax of the book takes place in one of the side
chapels of the Temple of materialism, where Sherry, who has
dropped out of school, has taken a job as a store assistant in order
to provide Rod the anarchist monster with a place to plant his

bomb. And he does rescue her, but—here my story follows Neuman rather than Frazer—in the process passes beyond his need for her to achieve his personal salvation.

Once again I have made the structure of my book and the process of arriving at it a great deal simpler than it in fact was. But apart from this I'd like to mention two particular problems it gave me. The first was a problem which in one form or another must face most writers, even though they normally overcome it instinctively. Whereas in *High* I was writing from the point of view of an Englishman—one who knew quite a lot about America but might make errors, and even more important one who could be assumed to be presenting his material for an English reader who was no better informed—the same assumption couldn't be made in *Generally A Virgin*. Here I was using Jo's point of view, and it seemed quite wrong that this should in the same way make concessionary explanations for foreigners.

As a result I set myself the difficult task of writing as if for Americans, using American allusions and American words. At first indeed I attempted a kind of colloquial argot in the narrative as well as the dialogue, though later I rewrote it throughout, retaining the best I could do for American dialogue but using a less slangy though still American style for the narrative. The result, I suspect has been ironic: it succeeds sufficiently well to convince an English reader but not some Americans.

I say this is a general problem not because many English novelists will try to write about America but because they must all have in mind whatever they write about, some conception of their reader, a suggestion which seems obvious when you consider whether you would use the same style and vocabulary in an account designed for a university don, a road-mender or your ten-year-old son. I mean no disrespect for any of these classes, it is merely a question of communication and sympathy. Most writers automatically assume that they are writing for their friends—I certainly do—and leave it at that until some problem like my American one makes them think about it.

The second problem concerned the book's structure. When all was completed and written I felt that in the process of getting it to fit my plan I had somehow killed it. I had to take the whole book and as it were give it a great shake to make it fit less exactly and neatly, or rather to restore to the characters something of the spontaneousness, the life-like but untidy impulsiveness, which they had lost. The necessity to give my book this life restoring shake confirmed my determination never again to write a book in

which I knew so clearly what I was doing, but to leave questions
of myth, allegory and symbolism—to mention just a few—to the critics, to whom they properly belong.

Here I will stop. I hope I have given you an idea how just one
writer has tried, as the organizer of this series so flatteringly put
it, 'to extend the frontiers of his medium'. In concluding I wish I
could show the three books I've been talking about as some sort
of pattern or logical sequence of experiment, but I'm afraid that
that isn't the way they seem to me, however they may seem to a
critic. Instead I see them as three quite separate attempts to
branch out from the main flow of the realistic novel, the sort of
attempts many novelists make, some of which work, some of
which don't. Almost the only connection to me between my spy
story and my two American novels is that all three sprang as
much from technical ideas about the novel as from experience.

If there is one thought I would leave with you it is this. I
believe in such experiments. But I think they are unlikely to succeed if they are merely experiments for their own sake. The
success of an experimental novel, I suggest, depends finally, like
every other novel, on its guts, on the real feelings about real experience which *also* go into it. It is only when the experimental
form or style match these, when it is the best possible, perhaps
the only, way to communicate them, that the frontiers of the
medium will be truly and successfully extended.

HUMOUR:
THE MODERN RELIGION?

PAUL JENNINGS

Read 17 April 1975:
J. W. Lambert in the Chair

ALL writers worth their salt, unless perhaps they are Dickens, hate the dreadful white empty page, the obscure feeling that they are not going to have enough time (what am I saying, 'obscure'? The only too clear feeling), that they wouldn't have enough time even if they had all the time there was, to make the perfect, irrefutable shape. Various people, many of whom they will never meet, will handle whatever it is they have finally typed out, obscure but powerful personages will append little notes displaying judgment, acumen, commercial sense, Eng. Lit. degree, etc., as it passes about in offices, in-trays, large buff envelopes. Then, unalterable, unrecallable, it will become the concern of brown-overalled men in printing firms, in buildings that passers-by are still vaguely surprised to observe as in the modern-impersonal style, in unlikely places such as Letchworth, Herts., or Bungay, Suffolk. Choose from the infinite howling void, get it right, quick, quick, everybody's waiting . . .

This is bad enough if one is merely making the dreadful, irreversible choice of what happens to characters in a novel or play, both of which I have written, as well as the short humorous pieces on which my life and overdraft have been based, and about which I get nice letters from people saying how much they laughed when they got them out of the library.

The novel was published, slightly fazing metropolitan, pigeon-holing batch reviewers by its flippant treatment of a desperate, serious subject, television (since I agree with the great Thurber, of whom more later, that 'the true balance of life and art, the saving of the human mind as well as of the theatre, lies in what has long been known as tragicomedy, for humour and pathos, tears and laughter are, in the highest expression of human character and achievement, inseparable'). Mr Jennings is or was a well-known humorist, they said, Mr Jennings is a logodaedalist, good heavens he has written a novel (100 of their 200 words gone already), good heavens some of it is serious, good heavens there are no dirty bits, perhaps Mr Jennings is too nice . . . actually the further north the better the reviews, splendid in the *Irish Times*, best of all in the *Scotsman*. It ought to go like a bomb in Greenland.

The play has never been done, but people's reasons for turning it down, from the RSC through the Abbey, Dublin, to the Mercury, Colchester, are so wildly different and often totally contradictory that I'm sure it will be done one day, when Talking comes in again and Actors' Significant Silences are out at last.

But I digress. What was I saying, ah yes, What Is Man? No, I wasn't, I was saying how particularly absurd it is to suggest that the writing of humour, *any* kind of attempt to equate its creation with that of any other form, is worthy of the same analytical effort that other forms most certainly get. Who would dream of writing an opera, for instance, without a double-page spread in the *Observer* about the difficulties of its conception and gestation? (Mozart, that's who.)

The fact is that any good humorous writing ought to look as though the man who wrote it was out there in the real world, doing something real, actual, extrovert, masculine—digging a ditch, building a suspension bridge, winding an armature, gelding a horse, picketing some power station, or whatever—and suddenly this divine idea flashed into his head; cackling with laughter he rushed upstairs and typed it out in about ten minutes.

Another fact is, however, that this happens about twice in the writer's lifetime. I start (and indeed end), therefore, with a paradox.

On the one hand I believe that the encapsulating of the comic *in print*, not in the mouths of TV actors, brilliant though many script-writers are (and what bright young man could be blamed for seeing his future there, not in the ever-decreasing field of journalism; who would now say his ambition is to write a humour column?) is just as worth while as writing serious novels or poetry or criticism, indeed *more* worth while than most criticism except that of George Steiner, real didactic, leading-you-on criticism. And George Painter, of course. And L. C. Knights, and about three more.

After all, it is no small thing to be dead and to have left behind you writing, actual black marks on a white page, which can elicit a physical response, laughter—like its opposite, weeping, involving breath, life, a real movement of the body. Of course nothing is more personal than humour. How often has someone said of one of my own pieces that his wife nearly choked over her coffee while reading it (hooray) to be followed almost immediately by someone else confiding to me, with what *my* wife and a school friend years ago decided was their least favourite quality in anyone, that of *engaging frankness*, that 'it wasn't up to your usual standard' (sob). All I can do is to give two examples of pieces by men now dead which can still evoke physical laughter from me however often I read them.

In *For Love and Money*, a collection of pieces by Paul Dehn, like most good humorous writing long since out of print, there is a divine article in which he demolished the whole ridiculous, inflated Mitford U and non-U thing by the simple expedient of commenting on her U and non-U versions of the same thing as defined in the *O.E.D.* Very often its reading aloud to dinner guests has to be abandoned because everyone is laughing so much. If it makes the present reader laugh he will be the kind of person we should like to have to dinner. If not, not:

> What else do they eat between meals? '*Sweet*', says Miss Mitford, 'is non-U for U *pudding*'.
> **Sweet** Middle English 1. That which is sweet to the taste; something having a sweet taste. b. A sweet food or drink.
> **Pudding** Middle English *poding*, deriv. unkn. I. 1. The stomach or one of the entrails of a pig, sheep or other animal, stuffed with minced meat, suet, seasoning, etc., boiled and kept till needed; a kind of sausage. 2. Bowels, entrails, guts. II. 1. A preparation of food of a soft or moderately firm consistency, in which the ingredients, animal or vegetable, are either mingled in a farinaceous basis, or are enclosed in a farinaceous crust, and cooked by boiling or steaming. Preparations of batter, milk and eggs, rice, sago, suitably seasoned and cooked by baking, are now also called puddings.
> It will not, I assure you, be pleasant—as I traditionally eat my

sweet food and drink my sweet drink—to think of these hirsute, half-naked, Transcaucasian Mitfords spooning up great helpings of batter, rice and suitably seasoned sago or (at worst) of guts, entrails and even bowels cooked by steaming. And where, I should like to know, did they find the pigs whose stomachs they stuffed and kept (under their straw pallets?) till needed? In one of our family sties, no doubt. Tartar nomads who live furtively in 'portions of buildings designed for cattle' are not immune from such temptations.

What do they do when they have finished their savage meal? '*Serviette*', says Miss Mitford, 'is exaggeratedly non-U usage for *napkin*' . . .

As it happens, you could apply some boring 'social criticism' tag to this wonderful piece. But I believe that Humour is a much larger and at the same time purer concept than Satire, that somewhere out there is the Platonic Form of the humorous; the perfect Joke, pure humour, just as valid a notion as pure goodness or pure truth or any other of Plato's Forms. And my next quotation, from a piece by A. P. Herbert (whom I would much rather have had to dinner than, say, D. H. Lawrence) speaks for itself:

the typewriter to me has always been a mustery£? and even now that I have gained a perfect mastery over the machine in gront of me I have npt th3 faintest idea hoW it workss% &or instance why does the thingonthetop the klnd of lverhead Wailway arrange-ment move along one pace afterr every word: I ha Ve exam aaa ined the mechanism from all points of view but there seeems to be noreason atall whyit shouould do t£is damn that £, it keeps butting in: it is Just lik real life. then there are all kinds oF attractive devisesand levers andbuttons of which is amanvel in itself, and does somethl5g useful without lettin on how it does IT . . .

On the other hand (attentive readers will remember that way back in the eighth paragraph I said *on the one hand*) there is the undoubted fact that humour, of its very nature, is something that *ought* never to be defined. Any theorizing about it will produce something bearing about as much resemblance to the marvellous 'sudden glory' of laughter as the dead butterfly pinned out on the collector's board does to the live surrealist blob of colour blown improbably about the summer garden.

I once saw a piece in, I think, *Look* magazine (and I am never going to make Americans laugh, I see that now) called *The Crea-*

tive Agony of Arthur Miller. It was a big photo-spread, and there were pictures of him holding his head, frowning, bent double—even, if I remember rightly, writhing on the floor. Well, who wants to read about the Creative Agony of P. G. Wodehouse? And how many writers, however much Agony they endured, could write as well as he did?

Another paradox—'truth', as Chesterton observed, 'standing on its head to attract attention'. On the one (or, by now, the third) hand, 'the sense of humour' almost certainly comes at the over-sophisticated end of a civilization, the howling bearded primitive thugs who appear in a dust-cloud from nowhere to settle down and start it with a bit of farming aren't usually great laughers. As Stephen Potter wrote over twenty years ago, 'a sub-era in the evolution of Englishness, in which humour has been regarded as an essential part of the Good, as a graceful and necessary congruity of social life, as something to be taken for granted as right, is beginning to pass away'. It sure is, as you realize every time you turn on the telly and there is some bespectacled strike leader saying why the lads think it is a diabolical situation.

On the other (or fourth) hand, the reductionism which now makes it compulsory for all literature, including poetry (indeed, *especially* poetry for some) to be considered as a department of politics, paralleled in religion by the smart de-mythologizing theologians like Bultmann and Küng, has, together with the boring, anaesthetizing effect of industrial civilization, made humour change. From being a fundamentally human but chance, here-and-there, casual phenomenon it has become a fundamentally human but organized, vital-to-sanity and prestigious *necessity*. Any day now Spike Milligan ('well, folks, any man can be 62, but it takes a bus to be 62A') will have created for him the title of Anarchist-Royal, and quite right too.

Fundamentally human? Of course it is. You could almost define man as 'a laughing animal'. People who show pictures of their dog and say 'Look, there's Rover laughing' are, aptly enough, barking up the wrong tree. You need an intellect to be able to laugh. I mean this not in the sense it has come to acquire, of being equipped with a conventional book-culture, or even in Virginia Woolf's sense of being ready to chase an *idea* up hill and down dale. I mean it in its original derivative sense, from *intus legere*, to take in. For humour involves the unique ability of the human intellect to hold, to take in, a simultaneous variety of wildly differing concepts; the same quality that enjoys metaphor in poetry.

One way of looking at it (and do remember that this is probably all tosh, it's only *my* way of looking at it) is to think of all these concepts as horizontal, laid out one after another sequentially in time, suddenly brought together with divine unexpectedness in the vertical, instant lightning flash of laughter.

Thus: years ago I remember laughing, and I never forget anything that has made me laugh; I remember a piece by Nigel Balchin in *Lilliput* describing ideas sent in by the public for 'beating the bomber' during the Blitz. He was at the receiving end in some Ministry or other. Most of the ideas, he said, were either crazy, such as 'Why don't you freeze the clouds and put anti-aircraft guns on them?', or else they had a minute grain of scientific feasability but would involve considerable diversion of the country's war effort and were usually some kind of death-ray machine such that 'if you could get a German soldier to stand perfectly still in front of it for twenty-four hours, *wearing a copper waistcoat*, he would feel *pretty seedy*'. My italics, unnecessary really. I remember Peter Fleming criticizing the performance of Sir Cedric Hardwicke, brought over at enormous expense to play Dr Faustus; 'Faustus has consorted with Helen of Troy, ridden on the backs of dolphins and savoured innumerable delights; he now looks forward with terror to the doom of an intolerable perdition, and it is simply no good to play this part as though he were a retired detective-inspector having a flutter on the black market.' I remember Monsewer Eddie Gray saying . . .

What am I doing, trying to wrap such divine gifts in the dismal brown paper parcel of some theory or other? Ah well, let's begin the preceding paragraph again. Years ago I remember, on the *Charivaria* page in the old *Punch*—same cover every week, no rot about topicality or theme, just a heroic attempt at the impossible, eight pieces of pure humour a week, greeted, then as now, by people who say with the air of one making a witty and original statement that they only see it 'at the dentist's'. They should be so lucky. All my dentist has is very old copies of *Autocar*, or something, and what was that publication called, ah yes, the *Sunday Times Magazine*.

I shall get to this in the end. Years ago I remember seeing, on the *Charivaria* page in the old *Punch*, a snippet from some women's magazine:

> Your cupboard must have been too moist, or too hot. Do not, however, throw the jam away. Scrape off the mould, and use it in jam tarts and puddings.

Under this was *Punch*'s comment: '*Then* throw the jam away.'
Readers who don't think that is funny will now kindly leave
this essay. For those who remain I should like to lay out (sequentially, horizontally, etc., see *supra*, as the learned men say)
some of the concepts here 'taken in' by the intellect.

1. The concept of someone solemnly scraping the mould off
mouldy jam and actually making mould tarts.

2. The concept of throwing the jam away. Is there not somewhere at the back of your mind the idea, not so much as of the
jam being thrown away in whatever contained it, as of the
thrower with jam actually on or in his (or more likely her)
hands, stuck between the fingers, needing a tremendous wrist-
flinging motion, before the residual stickiness can be got rid of
by mere washing?

3. The concept that the word *jam* has in itself, for mysterious
reasons, the germ of funniness. You can write the word, all by
itself on a piece of paper, thus:

jam

and (certainly if you are a humorous writer, a profession I do not
recommend, because *nobody listens*) the more you look at it—

JAM

—the more curious possibilities seem to uncurl from it. This does
not happen with many words. *Ceiling, reason, notepaper* . . . you
could look at inert words like that for ever and they would still
simply be *ceiling, reason, notepaper*, with no associations. But
jam, a *jam* factory—well, consider the effect achieved by Lewis
Carroll by the simple expedient of substituting *jam* for *wine* in
one of those solemn tastemanship pieces (in *Sylvie and Bruno*):

'Not for *all* qualities!' an eager little man shrilly interposed.
'For *richness* of general tone I don't say it *has* a rival. But for
delicacy of modulation—for what one may call the "harmonics" of
flavour—give *me* good old *raspberry*-jam.'

'Allow me one word!' The fat red-faced man, quite hoarse
with excitement, broke into the dialogue. 'It's too important a
question to be settled by Amateurs! I can give you the views of
a *Professional*—perhaps the most experienced jam-taster now
living. Why, I've known him fix the age of strawberry-jam to a
day—and we all know what a difficult jam it is to give a date to—on a
single tasting! Well, I put to him the *very* question you are discussing. His words were "*cherry*-jam is best, for mere *chiaro*-

scuro of flavour; *raspberry*-jam lends itself best to those unre-
solved discords that linger so lovingly on the tongue; but for
rapturous *utterness* of saccharine perfection, it's *apricot-jam
first and the rest nowhere!*" '

We are practically in *Monty Python* country here. *Jam* just is a
funny word. According to the *O.E.D.* it is derived from the perhaps onomatopoeic verb 'to jam'. Certainly, with its monosyl-
labic, quasi-Saxon bluntness, it joins the company of words like
fish, blob, hat, glue, sock, boot, thump, pudding, golosh, treacle—
words which come over and over again in the work of the in-
comparable Beachcomber. Thing-words, perhaps, contrasted
with the abstract Latin-based words, like *reason, urbanity, pro-
crastination*, which go into the rich amalgam of English. Maybe
the funniness-potential of such words goes right back to the
sophisticated sniggering of Norman courtiers at the rude language of their Saxon hinds . . .

I don't know. What I do know is that about 700 words on from
the original joke, *then throw the jam away*, I can still be formulat-
ing some of the concepts that were, consciously or subconsciously, involved in it, in the instantaneous laugh.

This may prove to some, if proof were needed, in Beachcomber's phrase, that theories about humour are very unhumorous.
Why shouldn't they be? As readers of a proper book like this
one (i.e. never seen in the standard English bookshop, among all
the showbiz memoirs, pornographic magazines, car instruction
manuals and gift candle-holders) will know without my telling
them, better men than me have produced 'intellectual' theories of
humour. Bergson thought comedy arose from the rigidity of the
human body and character, considered as part of the brute
change-resisting world of matter, opposed to the divinely pliable
spiritual *élan vital*. There is always comedy when people have
ossified, solidified, into habit or type, the classical French com-
edies are actually often titled after psychological types—*L'Avare,
Le Misanthrope, Le Bourgeois Gentilhomme*, etc.—whereas tragic
titles are usually an individual name—*Phèdre, Antigone, Macbeth*.
Tragedy is internal, comedy is external.

Then there is Freud, and there is the standard 'cruelty' theory,
according to which you enjoy seeing the man fall on the banana
skin. I don't enjoy it at all, I can feel quite sorry for him emotionally while intellectually I am laughing. And my several-con-
cept theory fits the case just as well. On the one hand, the concept
of the vertical, dignified person, pompous—a company director, a

trade union leader or whatever. On the other (and I absolutely promise there won't be any more hands in this piece), there is the concept of the same person suddenly, inexplicably, divinely *horizontal*—the last idea that was in your mind until he actually stepped on the banana skin. The humour is in their amazing and instantaneous juxtaposition in the mind, in the *intellect*.

'It's all in the mind, folks,' as Spike Milligan used to say in another context. Well, the same context really. So it is. It's no accident that modern humour, closely connected with surrealism, should have reached its highest point in radio, in the immortal *Goon Show*. There is no visual surrogate for a line like 'Open the door and let's get this room in.' Surrealism also is instantaneous, it also involves the bringing together of utterly disparate ideas, and the bringing together happened in five million (or whatever the *Goon Show* listening figures were) different ways in the intellects of its listeners.

The moment you put this modern surrealist humour on television you are up against strange, unavoidable limitations. The visual surrogate becomes strictly limited to that of one man, or at most the consensus of a production team, however brilliant (and they *are* brilliant); but certainly not that of five million (or whatever) viewers.

But something even more mysterious happens. It is absolutely no sort of comment on the respective characters of, say, Spike Milligan and John Cleese, to note that there was something open-ended about the anarchy of the *Goon Show*; something that approximated to Hamlet's 'There are more things in heaven and earth, Horatio / Than are dreamt of in your philosophy' *and* to Lewis Carroll's motif of the chessboard, which is either black squares on white or white squares on black. Reality is ambivalent to the mere human intellect, it is only unequivocally comprehensible to God, who, as St Thomas Aquinas remarked, sees complex things in a simple way, whereas we see simple things in a complex way.

Here we are straying into the whole theme of the dangerous magic of television, much better left to Marshall MacLuhan, like me a Catholic and unlike me a qualified intellectual boffin. But the moment people try, in programmes like *Monty Python*, to get all this into the strait-jacket of a visual conception, in a curious way that marvellous *instantaneity* of the surrealist modern joke is lost, an element of sitcom, of the half-hour slot, of the sketch, of realized characters, comes in; and because they are committed to surrealist unexpectedness none the less, instead of the magical *Goon*

Show feeling that 'there are answers, we don't know what they are, but they would surprise you and are happy in a wildly unexpected way', there is a strange kind of hardening into 'there may be answers, but in a cruelly unexpected world like this we are never going to know them, and, my God, it *is* cruel, isn't it!'

Let us leave all this to MacLuhan. Where does all this get us with written, *printed* humour? Does humour on the printed page share in the general movement towards what I can only describe as the enfranchising of humour today? By that I mean that laughter, which, I have now proved at least to my own satisfaction, has always been a fundamentally human attribute, and what is more, has always had its professional dispensers, from Aristophanes to Arthur Askey, has nevertheless been freed from some of its dependence on the observation of human character, funny enough though that is, God (literally) knows. For the old-fashioned kind of joke you often needed to people the stage as if for a one-act play; there was an Englishman, an Irishman and a Scotsman, etc. No such props are needed for the instant 'Open the door and let's get this room in.'

It is as though this kind of humour, a kind of magical crystalline globe, had got larger and larger, and finally grown into a whole 'other' world. And it is a world which people now expect to be *there*, they have come to expect their periodical, regular escape into it, because it is one of the few areas where the sense of wonder and surprise can be recaptured in a mechanized world.

The machine has reduced our sense of the otherness, the objectivity of the world. Wood which you have whizzed through with a circular saw is, so far as your experience of it is concerned, now as soft as butter. Distance and height have lost their magic. Every day marvellous silver aircraft sail over Mont Blanc and over celestial side-lit continents of cloud, sights seen by no man until this century except for intrepid Victorian balloonists, and by no man at all before them; and the people sit in their seats not looking out at all, reading *Playboy*, full of mechanical rubber girls, or the *Reader's Pre-digest*, if they read at all.

No doubt the physicist or biologist savours a delicious, life-enhancing intellectual terror as he peers into what he thinks is the heart of reality, the ambivalent dance between energy and matter—let alone the wonder of a proper philosopher, by which I mean a metaphysician, not one of those logical-positivist chaps trapped in their solipsistic cage of language, at the dance between body and spirit. But for most people life in an industrialized society means a diminution of the sense of wonder. Boring repetitive jobs are done by people living in boring architecturally repetitive suburbs and towns. The world has become a kind of giant boring Newtonian Meccano set (and oh, those dismal people in white plastic boots sitting at dismal consoles in cardboard space-ships, certainly no wonder *there*!). A world which does what it is told when you pull the right levers and switches.

So perhaps it is no accident that the two founding fathers should have been English. Lear and Carroll made an entirely valid, internally coherent cosmos of *absolute* Nonsense which was just as creative a reaction to the Industrial Revolution as was that of the Romantic poets; I am certainly not the first person to have observed that Lear's mournful long-vowelled cadences ('the great Gromboolian plain') can sound exactly like Tennyson's.

This was not only because Britain invented the modern world, but because even while she was inventing it she had doubts about it. We had the first railways but we had the first Luddites too. At the height of it all we were busy also perfecting the game of cricket, the exact and profoundly logical *opposite* of Industry, a beautifully organized way of doing nothing for sometimes three or four days: as classical as a Mozart symphony, six balls this way, six balls that way, yet with a deep regard for the quirks of human personality, everybody solemnly moving round for a left-handed batsman . . .

In other words, we were never fully committed to Industry, although we invented it, and are now the first to tire of it. But America, only recently overhauled by Japan, was the first society totally committed to mass-produced consumerism, selling, built-in-obsolescence, ruthless efficiency, etc. (She isn't now, but she *was*.) So it is even less an accident that the emergence not so much of pure Nonsense as of humour about actual life in industrial society should have occurred first in America, its finest, unsurpassable exponent being Thurber. No wonder the English recognized him, to the astonishment of Harold Ross, more than his own countrymen. *We* knew what he was on about.

If he had written only *Walter Mitty* he would deserve to be honoured for ever as encapsulating modern man in a story of barely 2,000 words. We have become used to long, long novels and plays about people In Search Of Their Identity. But Walter Mitty, stumbling through a Saturday morning in some industrial Nowheresville, lost in fantasies, got there first. In other ages you didn't need fantasies, you knew your position in society, you were a knight, a sailor, a rope-maker, a tailor, or whatever, in an ordered cosmos. It's beside the point here whether or not this cosmos was or was not itself a fantasy of tired-eyed, wise-unto-death, utterly illusionless people like Dostoievsky's Grand Inquisitor. The point is that there is now no shared world-picture, so people must make their own. If Faust was pure Intellect personified, and Don Juan was Lust personified, then Walter Mitty was Fantasy personified.

Who but Thurber would be half afraid that he might meet himself coming round a corner, or be followed by little men 'covered with blood, honey and the scrapings of church bells', or, without his glasses, see 'a gay old lady with a gray parasol walk right through the side of a truck'? Thurber himself quotes with relish the story of Max Adeler about the bridge-table which could be converted into an ironing-board, although the gadget which did this was very stiff at first; then it got easier, then it got so that if anybody just brushed it with their hip in passing it would change from a bridge-table to an ironing-board or *vice versa*, and in the end it had to be shut away in the attic, where it could be heard bumping away all night changing *itself*.

That kind of humour would have been unthinkable before industrialization. It is of the same genre as the Three Stooges film in which these lunatics descended on the same unfortunate house as gas, electricity, and water men. When they had done their worst, and departed, the owner of the house, tired after a long day at the office, came home, slumped in his armchair, and switched on the radio, from which promptly issued a gout of water (or it may have been flame, I forget now). Music came from taps, water from light switches, all the knobs and levers of our predictable mechanized world suddenly became very unpredictable indeed.

Modern humour with its strong surrealist element is, if you like, one way back to the sense of wonder. After all, babies are born full of wonder at the mystery of the universe. You have only to look at them exploring their own hands or toes, or the insides of handbags, or watching cats or leaves or clouds. The whole drug scene is perhaps a mistaken attempt to find wonder inside the skull instead of out there in the marvellous world, where it always has been and always will be.

In becoming, if you like, some kind of almost independently existing alternative wonderland, humour has become a necessity; and this means a necessity to *all*. If that sounds obvious, have a look at an Edwardian *Punch* and you will realize that humour was as strictly stratified into classes as society then was. In a way we have come full circle from the magical wholeness of my absolutely favourite play, *A Midsummer Night's Dream* (I'd go any-where to see a performance of it, by anybody—nuns, convicts, local rep, even London as long as it didn't have those Peter Brook trapezes, there's always a new depth to it). There you have the wonderful humour of the mechanicals in a marvellous synthesis with the sophisticated wit of the court, without envy on the one side or condescension on the other; it is true that Demetrius can make a sniffy upper-class crack like 'It is the wittiest partition I ever heard discourse' of Snout's Wall, but we have heard Thes-eus say earlier 'Love, therefore, and tongue-tied simplicity / In least speak most, to my capacity.'

The best in this kind are but shadows ... but, to tear myself away from that divine play, the point is that in a century or two rewards and fairies would have vanished, the mechanicals would have become faceless 'hands' in dark Satanic mills, the Court would have become a detached and fearful upper class; and this would all be reflected in humour. At the top, university wit—Wilde, Beerbohm. At the bottom, gutsy red-nosed music-hall. In the middle, Edwardian *Punch* with all the jokes about comic ser-vants, comic foreigners. 'Mary, I can write my name in the dust on this mantelpiece.' 'Lor' mum, eddication's a wonderful thing,' or words to that effect. (I do believe that there are people around who think *Punch* is still like this.)

And never the three would meet, one might have thought if one had been around in 1900. But, in humorous terms, they did, after two world wars and immense class upheavals. As usual, radio led the way. Perhaps the first humour to be appreciated and *needed* by all social and intellectual classes, from factory canteens to university common rooms, was ITMA during the war, dated though it may sound now (but that rattling door-handle, 'Can I do yer now, sir?' was certainly the precursor of 'Open the door and let's get this room in').

But when it comes to writing the stuff down, to be read by posterity, if there is any, will it last, is it really a separate art? *I* can't say. I can only suggest that there has been some kind of movement and development, as in any other art. I could use an-other 5,000 words to demonstrate from my own experience of writing a humour column from 1949 to 1966 (when the *Observer* decided that I ought to stop it and begin writing 'features' in 'well, the Magazine, the sports page, anywhere') that some people went along with this movement, but from the letters, at the begin-ning it was clear that thirty to forty per cent of the readers of that great paper thought I was part of the serious editorial content.

It finally trickled through to all of them that even if they didn't think it was funny, it was supposed to be (and *nobody* can make everybody laugh). I did a piece, for instance, about the true (!) meaning of English place-names. *Wembley* meant 'suffering from a vague *malaise*. "I don't think I'll go in to work today, I feel a bit wembley." ' *Thirsk* was 'a desire for vodka', *Kenilworth* was 'a beggarly or trifling amount; "he left her nobbut a kenilworth in his will" ', and so on. One letter began *Dear Sir, I have always been interested in the meaning of English place names, and was most interested in your article. I should be most grateful if you could tell me your sources ...* and continued with plenty of internal evidence that it was seriously meant, not a come-on.

Well. I have met people who don't think Beachcomber is funny. I have met people who don't think *anything* is funny. The fact is, many people go to an honoured tomb without a smile ever having crossed their faces. But history is too full of terrible men taking themselves with the utmost seriousness for me not to think that humour, and its articulation in whatever permanence is left to print, is ever more necessary.

Chesterton splendidly remarked, 'Seriousness is not a virtue. It would be a heresy, but a much more sensible heresy, to say that seriousness is a vice. It is a really natural trend or lapse into taking oneself gravely, because it is the easiest thing to do. It is easier to write a good *Times* leading article than a good joke in *Punch*.' (He can say that again.) 'For solemnity flows out of men naturally; but laughter is a leap. It is easy to be heavy, hard to be light. Satan fell by the force of gravity.'

At the end of the same book, *Orthodoxy*, he says '... the tremendous figure which fills the Gospels towers in this respect, as in every other, above all the thinkers who ever thought themselves tall. His pathos was natural, almost casual. The Stoics, ancient and modern, were proud of concealing their tears. He never concealed His tears; He showed them plainly on His open face at any daily sight, such as the far sight of His native city. Yet He concealed something. Solemn supermen and imperial diplomatists are proud of restraining their anger. He never restrained His anger. He flung furniture down the front steps of the Temple, and asked men how they expected to escape the damnation of Hell. Yet He restrained something. I say it with reverence; there was in that shattering personality a thread that must be called shyness. There was something that He hid from all men when He went up a mountain to pray. There was something that He covered constantly by abrupt silence or impetuous isolation. There was some one thing that was too great for God to show us when He walked upon our earth; and I have sometimes fancied that it was His mirth.'

We live (and perhaps are more surprised by it after the calm nineteenth-century afterglow) in a world always full of horror, of serious and terrible things. Worse than that, for the modern existentialist we exist meaninglessly, we have to make up our meaning, if any, as we go along (I wonder what Sartre thinks of Mitty!). Our being is contingent, poised ludicrously on the edge of non-being. The only Necessary Being is God (sorry, but there just isn't space to take on Oxford, and anyway they would beat me). But could it be that humour, as Thurber suggested, may yet save us? Can it be that the skull does not so much *grin* as roar with laughter at a divine joke of which we shall one day see the point, that

> In a flash, at a trumpet crash,
> I am all at once what Christ is, since he was what I am,
> and
> This Jack, *joke*, poor potsherd, patch, matchwood,
> immortal diamond,
> Is immortal diamond

My italics. Serious thing, laughter.

SHORT STORIES,
PERSONALLY SPEAKING

WILLIAM SANSOM, FRSL

V. S. Pritchett, CBE, D Litt, FRSL, in the Chair

I HAVE been asked this evening to speak about my own personal experience in writing short stories, and about any development or technical advance into new ground that I might have tried to achieve. Thus I am in the humanly happy, if questionably base position of being free to be absolutely self-centred for an hour, me talking about me. Other writers have different approaches to and methods with the short story—with these I am not concerned, I am here to analyse me.

And here this happy situation suffers already an adverse blow; for I am essentially a bad analyst. I am first and foremost an intuitive beast. Of course, over the years and the publication of eleven and coming-up twelve volumes of short stories, I have become conscious of many a matter of changing technique—but never, never have I been able to see clinically what makes a good story or an inferior one, which is really the essence of the problem. It is still a mystery to me. Nor can I judge by popularity or sales, because in several instances I can see that stories which happen to have a dollop of sex or violence in them, or romantic love, have sold better than others; *not*, absolutely *not* for my philosophical or ethical intention of writing the story, which I try to keep implicit in undertone, but for the purely arbritary carapace of romance, sex, violence which happened to be chosen to express my deeper intention. So, thus confessing that my subject tonight is much of a mystery to me, I am ditched from the start—and must simply content myself with giving you a few of the facts and my conscious attitudes, and leave it to you to be the detectives, the critical analysts.

First, I suppose, comes a statement of beginnings and back-ground. In this, I am a cliché—an only child, and in the manner of only children, often a lonely one. Leaving the child to create its own company—daydreaming, making up his own amusements, creating: creating myths, say from the furniture around him, or from the eavesdropped life as seen or heard three feet or more below the level of his elders' voices and expressions. So, early on, one becomes an old hand at the ability and urge to create. At the same time, I believe there is a lot of the parrot in the human make-up, the copyist—what is more politely called 'being influen-ced by'—and thus with omnivorous reading of such material as the then *Boy's Own Paper* and *Strand Magazine*. I found myself urged to write down, rather than only daydream, my myth mak-ings; and I still have several of what were very many blood-curd-ling yarns scribbled down at the age of something like eight to ten, as far as I can remember. There was also a 'book'—I did not consci-ously think in terms of 'novel'—begun at the age of eleven: only the first chapter was written . . . no staying power, or the intervention of school? I shall never know.

At the same time, I was either born with or early came by an ability to draw with some facility. My father was a naval archi-tect, and a Sunday painter—a pretty good one. He also used to draw portraits of his friends, accompany these with jingling, witty small verses—and sometimes, on the occasion, say, of a local billiards tournament in the suburban Streatham where we lived, get these printed into a little booklet to be given to those inter-ested. So here was also a most material vision of creation at work. Consequently, I also drew a lot, and made up my jingles, many, many of them, as the years dragged on. Then at thirteen or four-teen, I got bitten by the jazz bug (this must have been stimulated earlier, musically, by an old pianola on which my parents used at jovial times jovially to play jovial tunes—making music a 'happy' thing) and both played the piano and began composing. All this left me, at the age of eighteen or more, with vague wishes to be either a composer, a painter or a writer: so I went into a bank. That is, my father got me into one, nepotically as was so usual in those days, to travel the departments and growing to be a beauti-ful banker. I complied docilely enough. A middle-class background spoke only of selecting some such career—the professional world of the arts was something godly and remote. But the amateur world still existed, and I went on creating, largely words and music, seeing myself one impossible day as a sort of Noël Coward *and* designing the sets. Four years in the bank; then, to make commercial use of my persistence in writing, into an advertising agency as copywriter. There by good chance a colleague was the poet Norman Cameron; we became friends, he introduced me to other poets like Dylan Thomas, and from these and their exhilarating, myth-making conversation I soon learned that literature is no remotely divine and inaccessible affair, but instead lively and real and all around us. But not until the war years, and I was twenty-eight or twenty-nine, did I write down, seriously and for myself and no audience, a short impression of my then nightly life, fire-fighting in the London docks. Quite by chance, it got into Cyril Connolly's hands, and was published in *Horizon*. I was flabbergasted. My little words, alongside those of the still professionally distant élite! Flabbergasted, but not knocked off my perch, rather—on to it. I think it was then that I concluded, rightly, that one should write what one really wants to, and not what one thinks a mass readership requires. (I had, in previous years, written quite a pile of 'formula' magazine stories, all of which had been rejected.) Then—chance again. Stephen Spender was posted to our fire-station, and he urged me to send some of my current stuff to John Lehmann and *New Writing*. Again acceptance! My inhibitions abated, on leave days I wrote and wrote; and before the war ended had two books of short stories to my credit—and, again chance, I mean credit, for that was a time when people read a lot, there was nothing else to do, no cars or television to play with. Circulations were large, I was set on the road.

From all this I can see first how slowly I got there, from the chrysalis of a fairly ordinary golf-and-guinea-conscious middle-class suburban background with its philistine rules; but also how I seized every opportunity of contact with the arts—one can never stress too much the importance of being alive to this seizing—and how doggedly persistent I was over all those slow years, often, as with the formula magazine stories, in the wrong direction. In passing I must add that, apart from school, I never had any academic training in the sense of 'studying Literature'; I simply read and read what I wanted to. I never forced myself to take medicine which was likely to do me good. How I graduated from potent but cheap novels to those written in strong, good prose I shall never know—possibly a musical ear, possibly even an unsuspected brain-wash of classically ordered Latin during school years, possibly the borrowing of books from people I respected. Anyway, in my early twenties I was well on the way with Rilke and Montherlant, Chekhov, Kafka, Virginia Woolf and others—none of whom I can claim was a special influence, a writer is seldom conscious of exactly who has influenced him—at least, that goes for me: with the exception, perhaps, in my earliest work, of Kafka; but then there was much Kafka in the air at the time, early Isherwood, Edward Upward, Rex Warner all producing works of strictly embodied fantasy-with-its-feet-on-the-ground of a Kafkaesque feel. But that is long ago—though I note that in my stories I still tend to choose a single-syllable name for my main character, and often strike off in a mysterious, not *quite* of this world manner. But apart from this, long, long ago I left Kafka. Today I want to be very much down to earth, and above all economic of words—an endemic purple pen is my worst enemy, to whom, alas, I do from time to time, and *consciously*, dammit, give in. I try also to be implicit rather than explicit, to impress soundlessly and subtly my intention; no preaching—on the basis that what is unwritten, and hovers between the lines, is a writer's strongest content. In all, I have no great message to impart, and I am not, in the usual sense of the word, committed. I hope I am much more broadly committed—to the broad illumination of everyday or out-of-the-way human activity and feeling and thought. In this I think that technically my way is to make the ordinary seem extraordinary—or of intense wonder or beauty, if you like—and to make the extraordinary seem not exactly 'ordinary' but certainly possible, probable, palatable.

'And how do you go about this?' comes the question. First, the superficial sides, and the absolutely unimportant question, do you *do* it on a typewriter or do you actually write it? What on earth difference should it make? If anyone *must* have an answer, I write it in longhand, because I enjoy the feeling of the pen (like drawing), and I can take my exercise book out into the garden if it is a nice day, and I dislike machines and their noise. The second question is always: 'Do you work on inspiration, or do you keep office hours?' More important. I work regular hours, often with limitless overtime; and certainly through Saturdays and Sunday mornings, and the mornings if on 'holiday'. Also I keep these hours if there is no particular plan worked out—faced with the blank paper something may start one off. I'm never afraid, as many writers say they are, of the blank paper; on the other hand, it entices me, I feel I must make my mark. Should such long hours seem too Spartan—and you can add the business side of letters and of selling, research and proof-reading—it leaves one free to take a day off when really needed, and not dictated by the chimera 'week-end'. I think it is also vital for a writer to keep social commitments to a minimum, so that at least he is free to write, face the white page.

But now to matter of much more pertinence—how does the story itself come about? With me, usually by stages. First, at some time there occurs a general theme which should be worth writing about—usually from my own experience, but often from some chance remark about somebody else's which has set me wondering: 'What would I do in similar circumstances?' Thus, for instances, the theme might be jealousy, or the going and coming of physical courage, or the division between thrift and meanness, or . . . etc. This theme is then stored, perhaps for months, years, in the back of my mind. Then, at another time, I find myself in some place or weather situation which I know I will want to describe in words—say, the mysterious essence of estuary country, the magic of salt and fresh water meeting, the eerie flatness of mud and sandbanks. Or it might be a corner newspaper-and-tobacconist shop—and I think, how many, many of these I have passed in my life, one day I must get down to putting its character exactly on paper, bring its oddnesses and personality to life. And into the back of my mind goes an intriguing background. Then, people—the people who will enact the story. These are not likely, with me, to be based on friends or acquaintances. With such people I am either too absorbed to be clinically observant, or in shyness my defences are up and I am absorbed in absorbing myself. No good. With me, it is people I don't know, but in passing see, who become my characters. This or that person on a bus, in a café, on a train, anywhere; and their physique, and some nervous or other habit sticks: I have a picture of a person or persons which goes again into the store of the back of the mind. Then comes the day when the trigger is at last pulled—something happens to fire off the action. It might be something quite inconsiderable, like the action of a man about to retrieve a bag dropped by a passing and stranger woman—his pause, suggesting that if he touches the thing, he might be thought to be snatching it. 'Fascinating!' I momentarily think, and then with luck the computer works, and out click the remembered and stored characters, background and theme and fit precisely into the desired position. From this I rough out a plot, first facing up to the biggest problem of all, the suspension of disbelief.

The reader has got to believe you, from the word go, in the first few paragraphs. This can only be achieved if the writer himself believes. When I said just now that a kind of computer seems to click the various factors into place, I meant *without question*. Other stored factors might have been selected. But these exact ones come as if ordained, come naturally. More, really, than just a hunch. They are, in fact always are, very clearly visible on the cinema screen of the mind. They exist. And the writer has to know not only what he sees, but what all other details are. This follows. I remember the German novelist Heinrich Böll saying once that the *name*, particularly of his main character, was vital to him—before he got the name the character did not exist properly. Quite right. We all have names, definitively, and so should fictitious people to become solid as fact. Details of places, or rooms, should similarly be known. Not overmuch, but selectively enough. I personally never write about the place I am in. I always write about a remembered place. Because the memory digests raw material, and only retains the essentials. Writing, say, of a café in which I am sitting, by an Italian lake, various quite temporary features will be there in the arena of the eye's view, untypical elements, say a giant blue van drawn up, or a strange never-before-seen type of winged insect on the table-cloth, or a red-bearded priest or a moustached woman talking French—all these will obscure the ordinary detail, the way the sugar is packed, the feeling and landscape of the lake, the typical kind of local passer-by and so on. These are the best remembered things of a place you know, not the residents of one hour.

I am lucky with my very visual mind in seeing my first scene extremely clearly. Now it is vital to sketch in, in the first paragraphs, as much sensuous truth as possible—using colour, texture, taste, angle of light, weather, one predominant human action and so on—all to solidify the scene quickly, to make the reader's own intimate senses respond and believe. Also, some sense of the showman in me likes to have, if possible, an arresting first line—a kind of fanfare as the curtain goes up to shock the reader into attention. Thus, at random I can remember, for instance, the sentence, simple, 'Snakes occur.' Full stop. Or: 'Two fishmongers were stretched sweating in deckchairs in their back-yard.' Or: 'It was the opposite to falling in love at first sight; at their first meeting he hardly sighted her at all.' Or: 'His name unknown, he had been strangling girls in the Victoria district.' There 'the Victoria district' is a solid detail worth hundreds of lines—also that 'unknown' about the man's name is provocative. In general reference, perhaps the simple words: 'Once upon a time' used in fairy stories are the most important four words—to make fact of fiction—ever devised. You can't use them with a modern story—but I got near it once by beginning: 'Once a young man was on a visit to Rome.' Something precise, succinct, not to be argued with about such a definite statement. It usefully came, in this case, straight beneath the title, which was 'A Woman Seldom Found'.

This brings me to the bedevilling question of titles—of short stories, and worse, of novels. Writers tend to play about for some delicious, tongue-tasty poetic phrase. Or apt quotation from the classics. I have learned, through long experience, that this does not work well. It is vital simply to state what the story is about. How very often I have had strangers come up to me and say: 'How very much I loved (loathed) that story of yours—I forget the title—about the man who ... etc.' I call to mind one about a witchy, bewitched girl on a Scottish pleasure steamer. All this was remembered by my stranger—but not the title. I had called it, nicely but uselessly: 'Gliding Gulls and Going People'. I should simply have called it 'Girl Bewitched' or something like that. I've got printed proof of this, too. I wrote a novel about a man falling in love with a woman seen in a window opposite to his. I wanted first to call it 'The Woman at the Window'. But played about, and finally called it by the nearish, but not near enough, and more luscious *The Loving Eye*. The book was translated into several languages: and with only one exception was called 'The Girl at the Window', or 'Through the Window' or 'From Window to Window'. You see? 'Window' was the real key.

But back to that all-important suspension of disbelief, which of course concerns not only the beginning of the story but the whole thing. I talked about the beginning just now, because it is as well to start early. Now once, thinking of this problem, I was reading Hemingway's *The Old Man and the Sea*. I liked the book. But as to any searching for a way to suspend disbelief—he had it all on a plate. Set in the Gulf of Mexico with its giant fish and its, at least then, poorly off but tough old fishermen—well, it was instantly believable. Could one, I thought, write a similar story about the solitary heroism of a poor old man in London? The idea tempted me. And a little later the computer worked and I came out with a long story sparked off by an old pensioner I happened to meet. He was an old chap who turned up to mend a few broken deck-chairs I had in a mousehole of a flat I lived in then. He worked there for some time. And I couldn't help noticing a suddenly joyful, bright look in his eyes, a happiness of whistling too, always on Saturday mornings. I asked him why. Instant answer: 'It's my day for making my weekly kate and sidley pud. Once a week I can go to it,' he said, 'and it lasts me the week-end, sometimes Mondays too.' This sank in. The importance of a bit of a humble blow-out when living on a small pension. Also, I had at times been in the rooms of the poor and pensioned in what was then 'Safe Old London'. And after a digestive while, Hemingway brought these to light—and I wrote a long story about the Old Man and The Pudding. I can't tell you all the details, but roughly it was the buying of the ingredients, the cooking of the steak and kidney pud—and then with it cooked on a plate, the old man slips on a bit of old fat and falls, breaking a thigh, and the pud goes slithering across the linoleum to the other end of the small tenement room. But a very long room to the wounded old man. Thereafter, for several hungry days and many detailed pages, I had him dragging himself inch by inch across that awful linoleum floor. Pain, hunger, purpose, survival—August, and friends away on their summer holidays. Plenty of detail, his worry about feeding the canary, more than himself even—and the visitation of a friendly old tom-cat off the tiles who jumps through the window and promptly eats half the pudding, without so much as a mewed 'hello'. People pass on the stairs outside—his weak cries can't reach them. He thumps the floor with his fist—an unseen voice outside the door says: 'Better not disturb him—he's at work mending something.' All that. Detail, detail, living detail—the suspension of disbelief. Finally, just when he's at long, long last near the pudding, his landlady comes in—picks him up and fussily makes him a cup of tea, leaving him still looking at the pudding, before he is taken off to hospital. I would have called that story, 'The Old Man and the Pudding'. But the word 'pudding' is too dangerous in Anglo-Saxon ears, too traditionally chuckle-making, like kippers and mothers-in-law. I called it simply 'Old Man Alone'—not quite on the mark. But—and this interests me—I was tempted to give it an awful trick title: 'The Prof [sic] of the Pud'— leaving the [sic] in. *And* making the old man a professor. But, you see, that would have been going against my computer, my already exactly seen scene. Tampered with like that, I feel pretty certain the story would not have achieved the life that fortunately it did.

I once read in a pamphlet from a 'writers' school' that on no account should one mention false teeth in a story. This prompted me almost immediately to write a longish story *only* about false teeth. It began with my central character in a dentist's chair with his first false teeth in for the first time, saying to his dentist: 'I feel like a cage in a bird' and went on from there—and it sold very nicely, thank you. Other challenges have been more dangerous—for they have been concerned with novels, thus risking, say, an average year and a half's work. Two instances concerned the usual novel's avoidance of what can truly happen, and often does, in real life. In *A Bed of Roses* I was impelled from the beginning to write a novel where the wrong man, an absolute beast, gets the right and charming girl. Another, called just *Goodbye*, analysed the break-up of a marriage of fairly long standing. Whereas usually in fiction, and in life too, the operative party, the divorcer, feels impelled to find a motive for her action, my main female protagonist came clean with herself and her husband by facing up to the fact that the marriage had become empty to her, it meant nothing any more, and that was that. As, I believe, happens very often in life—though usually the divorcer has to invent a more definite reason—exaggerating cruelty from simple rowing, or inflating a passing infidelity, or the suspicion of it. Again, and fairly recently, I realized that I had never written a novel from the point of view of a woman, told in the first person. 'All right,' I said to myself, 'I know a fair amount about women by now. I'll try and be one, on paper, for as long as it takes.' Of course, in these novels the backgrounds, characters and theme came out of the computered memory in the same old way: the impulse alone was in a sense artificial.

Now about plots, the plotting of my stories and, come to that, novels too. The theme dictates what essentially has to happen, and the end to which I weave. But the actual weaving I know only roughly. Set down a string of rough ideas on one piece of paper. The beginning, as I have said, is brilliantly clear. This would account for perhaps the first two or three printed pages. Thereafter—a truly joyful thing happens, something or other quite magically takes over, and I diverge from my original plan. The characters come alive and do what *they* want to do, not what I have planned for them. Other writers have recorded this—that the tale becomes only truly alive when the characters do, and dictate their own activities. Of course, it is not exactly magic, though it *feels* as if someone else above one's head is doing the work, and the writer is only an interpreter: but of course what the characters are doing are using the writer's own unpremeditated invention, and opening up hitherto sealed channels in the old computer of the memory. In any case, it is beautifully compulsive, nine out of ten times right, and saves all that itchy time, popularly glamorized, of the 'great' writer pacing his room, or the rough whizz-kid tearing rejected sheets from his noisy old typewriter. All that, at best, should not exist. The hunch is usually right, the first thought during the actual writing.

I shall illustrate this with an example. (*a*) The triggering-off. It was a pistol-shot cracking the quietude of Acacia Road, St John's Wood, N.W.8 on a fine spring morning. It was not a pistol-shot. It was a window-cleaner sportively cracking his leather. I looked through the window, and there was this man and his three fellow-cleaners shooting off a volley of flick-cracks at each other, grown men playing like children, a subject, very English, which always intrigues me. (*b*) Theme: the black windows, white-framed, of the three newish red-brick villas suggested emptiness and the emptiness suggested burglars. I had often pondered on what I would do if I met a burglar face to face, and the general mystery of the going and coming of fear or courage from day to day in the same person . . . so the window-cleaners would have to be cleaning one of the houses, empty, and find a burglar. (*c*) Unusually this was provided at trigger-point—though I had often before wanted to describe those non-entitous quiet villas set in their laburnum peace, they were in their very ordinary placidity a challenge. As such, they fitted a housebreaker very well. (*d*) Characters: an amalgam of several and many such independent 'working men' I had seen or known in the past. Plus the burglar himself, based on a top politician who is still alive and kicking, and might kick me if I mentioned his name.

So the story called 'Cops and Robber' began. I knew that after a few more playful antics—using their little ladders as pogo-sticks, etc.—one of them would meet a house-breaker, and that afterwards they would go into cautious conference as to what to do. Keep out of harm's way? Avoid at all costs being called as witnesses in a time-wasting court case? And perhaps he was armed? And so on. This, the thematic point, goes on during their café lunch together—when they are now all so nervous about it that more grown-up play begins. Finally, one with a conscience decides they ought to 'have a go'. In my rough notes, I had stressed that the housebreaker would have to be upstairs away from this morning life. And what better than being fast asleep—having stodged himself in the kitchen and wine-cupboard of an obviously empty house. He had been hungry—for I wanted later the window-cleaners to be ashamed of their triumphant catch. But lo and behold, having breakfasted and sniffed the weather one morning, and having got to work putting one of my men up a ladder to wake him, the man turns miraculously into the real owner of the house, whose wife has left him and to whom he has left the house; knowing her to be away, and still being in love with her, he has returned on the quiet for one more night, even if alone, on the bed of their broken love. Action now—I won't go into it, but the cleaners post themselves in military fashion at exits, one goes up the ladder to disturb the husband—and when at last he comes down . . . (another night intervenes for me, I had noted them cracking their leathers like a warning pistol-shot) . . . and next morning I start again and magically the tactic has changed to muzzling the man's head with one of those window-cleaners' little buckets. Much better, for now we have a strange headless figure standing dismayed by his own back door and surrounded by the ebulliently triumphant cleaners. Tears now from the bucket. The cleaners are discomfited. And then the husband, broken down, hopelessly confesses his unhappy love from the darkness of the bucket. The cleaners are confused, touched, and become all 'sir' this and that. They free the man, apologize and then drive off home in their van. The husband returns upstairs. (And I pack it in for the night. By now my notes have ended. I have not noted down any way of ending the story—hoping that it would take its own life on and find the way.)

As to endings generally, they must follow up some sort of final action, in which is implicit a tone of only temporary finality. Temporary, because no one is slaughtered, life will go on. I apply this regularly—no neatness, or trick ending, except for a final phrase perhaps. But certainly always the inference that life, as it does, could take one of a dozen new turns—since the characters are still alive. Call it no straight final line, but rather the completion of an oval—the egg to bear future life. In this case I came down the next day without an idea in my head—except that conscience would provoke anger in the cleaners themselves. But first the husband had to be dealt with. I made him return to the house, and do what I imagined an unhappy man in his circumstances might do, and I had done once in the past. I made him finger and love his wife's dresses in the wardrobe. Then a wicked thought came. Something I had not done, and which was certainly risking the suspension of disbelief. But the story had by then got far enough, I was feeling pretty certain of myself. So I made him dress up in one of his wife's ball-gowns, and waltz around the room. Innocently, emotionally, but dead-pan—no transvestite complication. And again he goes to sleep, in the dress. And the window cleaners? One of them calls on a good customer who tips badly,

gives him an insolent few pence to buy himself a lolly. Another
has his girl pinched by an Indian—whom he wants to punch up but
doesn't, because of his colour. The third pulls out a mantel-piece,
hits his wife with it, apologizes, spends the rest of the evening
painting the aggressive piece of wood 'a cheery gamboge'. The
fourth, an older man, takes things more soberly—leaves his wife
with the telly, goes out for his usual pint of mild, and goes to bed
hoping his arthritis and bowels will be better the next day. All, in
their different ways, have got the feeling of guilt out of themselves. Tomorrow, life will go on as before. As for the husband, the
wife comes back and finds him there, swears about the dress,
spends a last hopeful (for him) night with him, and the next day
packs a further suitcase to achieve the finest score in a wily
woman's way, to run off with his best friend. None of these five
directions had I imagined before sitting down and writing them.
They were arbitrary as life itself, chosen at random, choosing
themselves. Thus the most joyful manner of writing, when the
story takes over. Of course, the process is simple enough. For the
writer is not really in his room, at his desk. His imagination is
flickering somewhere quite else, in the scene of the story, right in.
Somewhere else altogether. In a world which makes itself up . . .
just perceptibly through his own consciousness.

A lovely freedom. But I myself am not quite free. I will not, I
hope, ever write about physical torture. I loathe it too much; and
hate its titillating potential. Also, I would hope to draw the line at
the darker side of hospital life. I've been in one or two public
wards now, and can see that if I wrote about the darker side, it
might just sink into the mind of a reader who is in future to be
not my patient but a surgeon's. Also, I do not write about the
intimacies of the sexual act. Sex is an animal-human act on a level
with eating; made humanly more complicated certainly, but basically, in terms of resportage, boring. To me Trimalchio's feast
was sludge compared with the brilliant rest of Petronius Arbiter's
book. In the same department I would place any gluttonous description of the moods of the genitalia. It would only be possible
for me if there was some collateral dramatic condiment—say, a
pheasant about to burn in the oven and in the woman's conscience, or even a lover under the bed. Otherwise, not from pris-
siness, but from boredom, for it seems we have heard or know
quite enough about the various contortions involved, I prefer not
to write about it. Also, I am a romantic in terms of the love of
men and women, and find the pre-sex play of endearment and
elation of much greater interest and subtlety. Also, the insertion

of a sexy chapter into a novel has become something of a vogue—often almost as if being written in by another and ghost writer to make the book sell—and I tend to shy away from anything in vogue.

I was asked particularly for this talk to speak of how I had broken or wished to break new ground in the matter of the short story. I can only repeat that I have not learned to do this by conscious or theoretical effort, but by learning from mistakes and adjusting myself to the pace of the times. Thus, I would not today write many of the long paragraphs of description which I wrote twenty years ago. Television, films, the proliferation of the image everywhere has taught me to speed up my matter; images do not stay still, even a static photograph suggests motion. At one time when the dropping of too lengthy descriptive passages became set in a novel, one critic suggested that I had lowered my sights to the writing of pot-boilers. How wrong he was, all the other old content was there, but he simply missed what perhaps he personally liked, an older-fashioned 'literariness'. (In this—I have never written either a 'pot-boiler' or for money: I write first, and afterwards long for the money, which I love for its gift of mobility and the leisure to write more, to follow.) I have learned also not to go for speed—which produces a bad nervous quick-reading gluttony—but for pace, quite a different thing. Pace, by setting short sentences against long ones, sudden poetic arrestations in clear prose—like describing a deep voice as the 'growl of a brown voice'. And so forth. I have learned also from the technique of modern publishing that what you write will not see the bookshop from the time it takes to write a book, plus printing and publication speed—for two and a half years! That is a real facer, with today's speed in the changing of fashions, slang-words, machine designs, etc. A writer must be very careful to generalize on clothes descriptions—in two and a half years, women may have all taken to veils or anti-mug helmets or painting their entire faces a different colour, men may be dressed in togas or kilts and wear feathers on their eyelashes ... who can tell? In this, it feels sometimes as if a censor is looking over your shoulder—with such quick fashion-changes, changes in the speed of aircraft, or, say, the so-modern hand telephone in a motor-car to a handless loud-speaker or even some device attached to the face by an ear-nose-and-throat specialist. You have to be careful. In this instance, the short story profits—it is published much sooner. And I have learned too about the short story that it is near to the poem, the writer can be immediately inspired and get the thing complete out of his system in a fairly short bout of intense work. The novel, on the other hand, is inhumanly long. Few other art-forms demand a similar year's imprisonment by the same subject: unless one is Proust, or painting the Vatican chapel's ceiling. I have also learned much about dialogue—that you can seldom transfer this directly from life, but invert it in some way so that intonation, impossible exactly to imply in writing, is at least sketched at. I have learned to rely on my musical ear for the going and coming, the echoing in a different key of themes and feelings. And from my painting ability to put not all of what my mind's vision sees of a scene, but rather a selection of the most forceful factors. In all these and other matters I cannot stop myself from sometimes cheating. Worst, is giving in to the purple pen. Otherwise, as an instance of giving in to the temptation to report exactly an unbelievable piece of dialogue, I was writing a little love story set against the background of a health farm my wife and I stayed at and I could not resist repeating words actually spoken to her in October by a nurse giving her a colonic irrigation: 'This'll clean us all right, Mrs Sansom—I want to hear those sixpences come tumbling out all the way back from last Christmas!'

I have lastly learned, probably among many other things, not to look for my 'influences'. One is often asked about this. No accurate answer can be found. It is all an amalgam of much, and of much that has probably been quite forgotten. But one can at least answer it the other way round, by saying what one hopes in the future may influence one, With me, it would be to have the tender but unsentimental humanity of Chekhov, the narrative ability of Maupassant, the prose-strength of Cyril Connolly, the characterization not of Dickens whom I find too chatty but of Evelyn Waugh or Somerset Maugham, the—what can I call it? —arrestation of Conan Doyle in Holmes mood, the mysterious economy of that sensuous major wizard called a minor Russian writer, Ivan Bunin, the pathos and dry humour of Jean Rhys, the complex play of words and outrageous fun of a contemporary young writer, Michael Feld, who should be better known than he is; and lastly the purity and quiddity of most of the poets of the Greek anthology.

Meanwhile, to paraphrase Rilke's beautiful prose-poem of Cornet Rilke, where the Cornet goes to join the army 'Riding, riding, riding / Riding, riding . . .' across the vast Pannonian plane—I shall go on writing, writing, writing across the vast penalized plane of the self-employed to the last horizon, so unlike my first *Horizon*, of the unpensioned—what, to end up a high-paid doddering butler in the U.S.? Potman in a pub? Old enough to be fatally mugged? Or to enter the queue for a twi-twi-twilight home . . . Still, it's a goodish life while it lasts, far freer than an eight-hour day week in and week out plomping the cherry in the middle of madeira cakes travelling a belt-line, as I know of one woman I met. And, apart from knowing that one's export earnings of hard gulden and dollars and francs go to bolster the lot of the not-self-employed, a social conscience may be gratified by the thought that one's work itself may be doing good, revealing life and widening the vision and sensitivities of those who can and wish to respond.

THE POET AS PAINTER

CHARLES TOMLINSON, FRSL

Read 16 October 1975:
Lord Clark, CH, KCB, C Litt, FRSL, in the Chair

'THE Poet as Painter' is not an altogether adequate title for what I want to talk about this evening. Although I can read to you from my poems, I shall not be able to show you my pictures. All I can do there, is to mention the appearance of a book of my graphic work, *In Black and White*, introduced by Octavio Paz and published by Carcanet Press. Perhaps some of you were even present earlier this year at my exhibition at the Cambridge Poetry Festival. What I shall be speaking of is chiefly the *materia* the poet and painter have in common. 'We live in the centre of a physical poetry,' says Wallace Stevens. This is surely the basic fact which would make a poet want to paint or, if he couldn't do that, to comprehend the painter's way of regarding the physical poetry they both share. It is because of this same basic fact of '[living] in the centre of a physical poetry' that Samuel Palmer's follower, Edward Calvert, could write of 'a good poem whether written or painted'. 'To a large extent,' says Stevens, 'the problems of poets are the problems of painters, and poets must often turn to the literature of painting for a discussion of their own problems.' One could add to this remark of Stevens that they not only turn to the literature of painting, but help create that literature. Stevens' *Opus Posthumous* has for its epigraph a passage by Graham Bell on the integrity of Cézanne, a painter Stevens has commented on memorably more than once. Besides Stevens, Rainer Maria Rilke, D. H. Lawrence, William Carlos Williams are all poets who have written penetratingly about Cézanne. All found in him a reflection of their own problems as writers as they fought preconception and subjectivity in their art. 'It is the crisis in these paintings that I recognized,' says Rilke, 'because I had reached it in my own work.' And D. H. Lawrence: 'Cézanne felt it in paint, when he felt for the apple. Suddenly he felt the tyranny of mind, the enclosed ego in its sky-blue heaven self-painted.' And Williams: 'Cézanne—The only realism in art is of the imagination. It is only thus that the work escapes plagiarism after nature and becomes a creation.' So Cézanne looms gigantically over literature as well as over painting, as the forerunner of a new sensibility and a new inventiveness. Indeed, Cézanne—to traverse the common ground between poet and painter in the other direction—composed many poems of his own. As a young man, he wrote:

> A tree, shaken by raging winds,
> Waves in the air, like a gigantic corpse,
> Its naked branches which the mistral sways.

As an old man, he made good this vision in an astonishing water colour that acquired the title 'Bare Trees in the Fury of the Wind'. Whatever the final product, the point of departure was the same: 'We live in the centre of a physical poetry.'

To Cézanne and his meaning for poetry I shall return. But, first, let me add to the title of my lecture, a subtitle, which will permit me to explore the centre of that physical poetry in which Stevens says we live. My subtitle is 'The Four Elements' and the place of my exploration, the Potteries where I was born. The element that touched most persistently on the imagination there of the child as a growing artist, was water. For that region of smoke and blackened houses, of slag-heaps, cinder-paths, pitheads, steelworks, had for its arterial system a network of canals. The canals brought back the baptismal element to a landscape by day purgatorial and by night infernal. The canals were not the only bringers of water into that place whose atmosphere, according to Arnold Bennett, was as black as its mud. One must not forget the great pools that formed in the pits where marl was dug for tile-making: as the pits were gradually abandoned, nature re-invaded, greenness appeared beside the water and fish in it. Fish! It was their existence, not just in the marl pools, but in the canals, that helped bring back contemplation into lives lived-out in the clatter of mines and factories. The fishing-club, the Sunday matches, long hours watching the rufflings and changes of water, something both sane and mysterious came from all this. Why mysterious? Because the fisherman, if he is to be more than a random dabbler, must acquire an intuitive knowledge of the ways of fish and water, and within his stillness, at the centre of his capacity to wait and to contemplate, there is a sense that is ready to strike at the exact moment, that even knows, perhaps, how to lure into its own mental orbit creatures that he cannot even see under that surface on which his whole attention is concentrated. Piscator is an artist, as Walton knew. His discipline, looking out from himself but with his inner faculties deeply roused, might make a poet or a painter of him if he had the latent powers within.

So much for water. What of earth and fire in this same Midland childhood? 'The district'—the Potteries, that is—says Bennett, 'comprehends the mysterious habits of fire and pure, sterile earth'. He means, of course, the action of fire on the potting clay. My own most remembered and most dwelt on experience of the physical poetry of fire concerns the making of steel rather than the making of pots. And it was an experience, principally, of fire by night. When the furnaces were tapped by night, or when molten metal was poured in the great open sheds of the steel works, immense dazzling shafts of fire flared outwards to be reflected in the waters of the nearby canal. Thus the remembered experience was also of fire associated with water, of fire not as the opposite of water, but mingling with it, kindling reflections in that element and also in the onlooker. To see was also to see *within*.

You gained this experience by following the canal beyond the factory established by Josiah Wedgwood in the eighteenth century, in the place named by him Etruria. You went on until the canal cut through the centre of the Shelton Bar-Iron and Steel Works. And you went by night, so as not to be seen, because children were not particularly welcome there. Etruria—Etruria Vale to give it its full name—had long since lost the nymphs one might associate with the name. But the red jets and glarings from molten steel, and from the furnaces seen in the canal, confronted one with a sense of the primal and the elemental such as nymphs themselves were once thought to symbolize in relation to landscape. And, after all, a dryad would only be a veil between yourself and a tree once your eyes had been opened by this other intenser nakedness. For, with the soot drifting down through the darkness on to your hair, you had experienced fire as the interior of water.

Earth, like air, fared badly in the district. 'It's atmosphere as black as its mud': Bennett's verdict. Earth, like air, took on the tinge of blackness. Earth was close to the sterile earth not only of pots but of slag-heaps and cinderpaths. For all that, gardeners coaxed miracles out of the sooty allotments that crowned the slopes where Etruria Woods had once flourished. As for air—air was something of a joke. There were local post-cards showing bottle-ovens and factory chimneys all smoking at once with dark hints of houses and perhaps a drab church-tower. These cards carried stoical titles like, 'Fresh Air from the Potteries'. At school, when the potteries 'stoked-up', it was sometimes difficult to see over to the far side of the playground. A familiar image returns from that time, of black smoke mounting from a factory chimney and, caught by the wind, fraying out across and into the air. Air was an element that yet had to be created there. It was, in part, the search for air, as well as water, that drew the fishing clubs out to the surrounding countryside, still along those canals, that seemed to lead back to Eden.

So of the four elements it was water that held the imagination of the child as growing artist—water fire-tinged, water promising a cleansing, an imaginative baptism, rocking, eddying, full of metamorphoses.

I left the district in my early twenties and subsequently lived among many landscapes both urban and rural—London, Italy, New Mexico, the northern United States, the Cotswolds. I think it was Liguria and Tuscany and then Gloucestershire taught me the way men could be at home in a landscape. And how necessary this different view of things was, in order to place those earlier experiences of streets that threatened to enclose you, to shut you off from a wider and more luminous world, from intuitions of what Ezra Pound calls 'the radiant world where one thought cuts through another with clear edge, a world of moving energies, magnetisms that take form . . .' I wanted to recover that 'radiant world' in poems, and by doing so I seemed to have lost touch with the Midlands. But the Midlands were always present as one term in a dialectic, as a demand for completeness subconsciously impelling the forms of one's art, even demanding *two* arts where the paradisal aspect of the visual could perhaps be rescued and celebrated.

Coming back to the Potteries almost thirty years later, I saw how much the world of my poems depended on the place, despite and because of the fact that they were an attempt to find a world of clarities, a world of unhazed senses, an intuition of Edenic freshnesses and clear perceptions. I tried to concentrate the history of all that into a short poem called

The Marl Pits

It was a language of water, light and air
　I sought—to speak myself free of a world
Whose stoic lethargy seemed the one reply
　To horizons and to streets that blocked them back
In a monotone fume, a bloom of grey.
　I found my speech. The years return me
To tell of all that seasoned and imprisoned:
　I breathe familiar, sedimented air
From a landscape of disembowellings, underworlds
　Unearthed among the clay. Digging
The marl, they dug a second nature
　And water, seeping up to fill their pits,
Sheeted them to lakes that wink and shine
　Between tips and steeples, streets and waste
In slow reclaimings, shimmers, balancings,
　As if kindling Eden rescinded its own loss
And words and water came of the same source.

Can my 'psychoanalysis of water', to appropriate a term of
Gaston Bachelard, point to any single prompting insight, any
happy combination of perception and intuition that unifies the
attitudes of poet and painter? Pondering this question, I remembered an early poem, 'Sea Change', formally quite simple in
that it seeks to catch the nature of water—this time, the sea—in a
series of images, 'uneasy marble', 'green silk', 'blue mud', then is
forced to concede their inadequacy: they are like

　　　　　　　　　white wine
　　　　Floating in a saucer of ground glass
　　　　On a pedestal of cut glass:

　　　　A static instance, therefore untrue.

Much later—the better part of twenty years later—in a formally
much more complex poem, 'Swimming Chenango Lake', I watch
a swimmer watching water. Here is an extract from the opening:

Winter will bar the swimmer soon.
　He reads the water's autumnal hesitations
A wealth of ways: it is jarred,
　It is astir already despite its steadiness,
Where the first leaves at the first
　Tremor of the morning air have dropped

Anticipating him, launching their imprints
   Outwards in eccentric, overlapping circles.
There is a geometry of water, for this
   Squares off the clouds' redundances
And sets them floating in a nether atmosphere
   All angles and elongations: every tree
Appears a cypress as it stretches there
   And every bush that shows the season,
A shaft of fire. It is a geometry and not
   A fantasia of distorting forms, but each
Liquid variation answerable to the theme
   It makes away from, plays before:
It is a consistency, the grain of the pulsating flow . . .

I pondered this passage, along with that earlier poem 'Sea
Change', to find out the constant that governed my attitude as
poet and painter. Poems based like this—as are the many landscape
poems I have written—on exposure to and observation of the fleeting moments of visual sensation; poems that endeavour to catch
this fleeting freshness and unite it to a stable form where others
may share in it; poems such as these look away from the merely
personal. And so does painting where the presence of the external
world is strongly felt, where the painter is concerned—I quote
Rilke on Cézanne—with 'the incarnation of the world *as a thing
carrying conviction*, the portrayal of a reality become imperishable
through his experiencing of the object'. To make the reality of
water imperishable! The painter must acquire great formal power
to achieve that: because he who looks into water, and into the
changing world of perception which water represents, looks into
the heart of time.

Cézanne himself was very conscious of this problem for the
painter—how to reconcile sensation and form without bullying your
picture into a wilful unity, a triumph of personality at the expense
of a truth to relationship: 'There mustn't be a single link too
loose,' Joachim Gasquet reports him as saying, 'not a crevice
through which may escape the emotion, the light, the truth . . .
All that we see disperses, vanishes; is it not so? Nature is always
the same, but nothing remains of it, nothing of what comes to our
sight. Our art ought to give the shimmer of duration with the
elements, the appearance of all its changes. It ought to make us
taste it eternally . . . My canvas joins hands . . . But if I feel the
least distraction, the least weakness, above all if I interpret too
much one day . . . if I intervene, why then everything is gone.'

Long before I read that conversation with Gasquet, I wrote a poem called *Cézanne at Aix*, a kind of manifesto poem where I wanted my poetry to take its ethic of perception from Cézanne, an ethic distrustful of the drama of personality of which Romantic art had made so much, an ethic where, by trusting to sensation, we enter being, and experience its primal fulness on terms other than those we dictate:

Cézanne at Aix

And the mountain: each day
Immobile like fruit. Unlike, also
—Because irreducible, because
Neither a component of the delicious
And therefore questionable,
Nor distracted (as the sitter)
By his own pose and, therefore,
Doubly to be questioned: it is not
Posed. It is. Untaught
Unalterable, a stone bridgehead
To that which is tangible
Because unfelt before. There
In its weathered weight
Its silence silences, a presence
Which does not present itself.

What impressed me about Cézanne, and what on my own humbler level I wanted for poetry, was the entire absence of self-regard. 'Cézanne's apples,' says D. H. Lawrence, 'are a real attempt to let the apple exist in its own separate entity, without transfusing it with personal emotion.' Cézanne must surely have felt the narrowing lure of what Lawrence calls 'personal emotion' here. Cézanne *in himself* was threatened by misunderstanding, neglect, ill-health and prone to deep melancholy. Had he chosen to ignore nature or merely to dramatise that self and impose it on nature, his pictures would have wanted the liberating Mediterranean radiance that we find there. Even his self-portraits lack introspection. Rilke, once more, supplies the classic comment. He writes to his wife: '. . . how great and incorruptible this objectivity of his gaze was, is confirmed in an almost touching manner by the circumstance that, without analysing or in the remotest degree regarding his expression from a superior standpoint, he made a replica of himself with so much humble objectiveness, with the credulity and extrinsic interest and attention of a dog which sees itself in the mirror and thinks: there is another dog.'

In speaking of Cézanne's incorruptible objectivity, it is clear that Rilke was not thinking of the purely imaginary and outmoded objectivity of nineteenth-century positivistic science—the objectivity which supposed a complete division between the observer and the observed. The objectivity with which Rilke credits Cézanne implied an outward gaze that would draw the sensuous world closer to the inner man and that would narrow the gap between abstraction and sensation, between intellect and things. As Merleau-Ponty reflects in his great essay, 'Eye and Mind'—an essay that begins by quoting Gasquet's book on Cézanne: 'Quality, light, colour, depth which are there before us, are there only because they awaken an echo in our body and because the body welcomes them . . . Things have an internal equivalent in me; they arouse in me a carnal formula of their presence.'

So much for Merleau-Ponty. I wanted to earn the right to use the artistic ethic of Cézanne as a basis for poetry, and I believe it made possible to me a range from natural landscape to civic landscape. It seemed to me a sort of religion, a bringing of things to stand in the light of origin, a way, even, of measuring the tragic fall from plenitude in our own urban universe. But let me make a confession. As a painter, I could find no direct way of using this inheritance. I confronted the four elements, but the only way I could resolve them in paint was to will their cohesion, to intervene, to put personal pressure on my forms in the shape of an anxious black outline. Time and again, I would approach the expression of some realization, only to disfigure it with black. I could find no way of letting the given suggest to me forms that could elude the preconceptions of the too conscious mind and the too conscious hand, blackening nature as surely as the factory chimneys of my boyhood had blackened it. Black became an obsession. Although I continued to draw, little by little I lapsed from painting, partly under pressure from this insoluble dilemma, partly because the time that might have gone to finding an answer went into earning a living. For fifteen years, almost nothing except the poems; then, in 1970, after a renewed, intensive spell of drawing, a solution appeared almost casually.

I think, once more, of Wallace Stevens, and that entry in his *Adagia* which reads: 'The aspects of earth of interest to a poet are the casual ones, as light or colour, images.' By 'casual', I take it that he refers to the fortuitous nature of art—the way one may find its deepest meanings on a dull street corner, in an old pair of shoes, in the chance conjunction of the totally unforseen and the apparently unrelated. Suddenly things knit up—the canvas joins

hands, in Cézanne's words. You cease to impose and you discover, to rephrase another aphorism of Stevens. And you discover apparently by chance. But what is chance? And if one
accepts it, does it not cease to be chance?

The element of chance that helped resolve my problems as a
painter was the surrealist device known as decalcomania. Briefly,
the recipe for this is the one drawn up by Oscar Domínguez in
1936: 'By means of a thick brush, spread out black gouache more
or less diluted in places, upon a sheet of glossy white paper, and
cover at once with a second sheet, upon which exert an even pressure. Lift off the second sheet without haste.' Well, the result of
this process, as the pigment separates out into random patterns,
can be a lot of wasted paper, occasionally a very beautiful entire
image, sometimes interesting fragments that prompt and defy the
imagination to compose them into a picture. You can alter what is
given with a brush, or you can both alter and recombine your
images by going to work with scissors and paste and making a
collage. The weakness of this technique is that it can lead to a
flaccid fantasy of imaginary animals, or of lions turning into bicy-
cles. Its strength lies in its challenge to mental sets, in the very
impersonality of the material offered you and that you must respond to. A very unCézannian undertaking, and yet what I have
called the ethic of Cézanne—submission to the given, the desire to
break with preconceived images of the given, the desire to seize
on and stabilize momentary appearances—this ethic, once applied,
can lead your decalcomania away from the arbitrariness of fantasy
towards the threshold of new perceptions.

I had followed Domínguez very literally: 'Spread out black
gouache,' he says. Max Ernst, using this technique for the basis
of some of his best pictures, clearly employs several colours.
Almost blindly, I reached for my old enemy, black. I continued
to use it and to use that colour only. The first move was to paint
the black on to a wet surface and the first thing you saw was the
strokes of pigment fraying out into the water just as the smoke of
your childhood had frayed out into the air. There seemed an odd
rhyme here between the one experience and the other. And as I
covered sheet after sheet, altered, blotted, painted with brush,
finger-tips, pieces of string, and then cut up and recombined, I
saw black become dazzling: I saw the shimmer of water, light and
air take over from the merely fortuitous: I saw that I was working
now as poet *and* painter once more.

The 'merely' fortuitous! *There* is a theme for them both: the
fact that 'chance' rhymes with 'dance' is a nutrifying thought for

either poet or painter. As is that other fortuity, that in the south
of England, they are pronounced 'darnce' and 'charnce', a source
of wonder to the Midlander, as no doubt *his* pronunciation is to
the southerner. There seems no intrinsic reason why these two
words should have much to do with each other. And there seems
no intrinsic reason, either, why the strokes of a brush covered in
pigment, the dabbing of a paint-covered finger, the dashes,
slashes or dots a painter makes, should have much to do with a
face, a landscape, a stone or a skull. Turner grew an immensely
long eagle's talon of a thumb-nail in order to scratch out lights in
his water-colours. It seems oddly fortuitous that these jabbings
into the surface of water-colour paper should come to represent
luminosity.

'Chance' undoubtedly rhymes with 'dance' and meditation on
this fact feeds the mind: chance occurrences, chance meetings
invade what we do every day and yet they are drawn into a sort of
pattern, as they criss-cross with our feeling of what we are, as
they remind us of other happenings, or strengthen our sense of
future possibility. Poetry is rather like this, also. Something seemingly fortuitous sets it off—a title, say, out of the blue, asking for
a poem to go with it, a title like 'The Chances of Rhyme' and you
find yourself writing on the back of an envelope:

> The chances of rhyme are like the chances of meeting—
> In the finding fortuitous, but once found binding . . .

Already, you have started to knit up those chances, with 'finding'
and 'binding' reinforcing the pattern and before long the chances
of rhyme are becoming the continuities of thought, and you continue writing:

> To take chances, as to make rhymes
> Is human, but between chance and impenitence
> (A half rhyme) come dance, vigilance
> And circumstance . . .

Yes, that makes sense. It seems to be getting somewhere: a pattern
in the words, a pattern in the thought, a pattern in the way the
line settles mostly for four main stresses, sometimes stretches to
five, mostly dances back to four. To handle measure thus seems a
human thing to do: your recurrences are never so pat as to seem
simply mechanical, your outgrowths never so rambling or bram-
bled as to spread to mere vegetation. A human measure, surrounded by surprises, impenetrable and unknowables, but always
reasserting itself, this could be a salutary aim—one in which rhythm

and tone are both allies—faced as we always are by the temptation
to exaggerate and to overvalue the claims of self:

The Chances of Rhyme

The chances of rhyme are like the chances of meeting—
  In the finding fortuitous, but once found, binding:
They say, they signify and they succeed, where to succeed
  Means not success, but a way forward
If unmapped, a literal, not a royal succession;
  Though royal (it may be) is the adjective or region
That we, nature's royalty, are led into.
  Yes. We are led, though we seem to lead
Through a fair forest, an Arden (a rhyme
  For Eden)—breeding ground for beasts
Not bestial, but loyal and legendary, which is more
  Than nature's are. Yet why should we speak
Of art, of life, as if the one were all form
  And the other all Sturm-und-Drang? And I think
Too, we should confine to Crewe or to Mow
  Cop, all those who confuse the fortuitousness
Of art with something to be met with only
  At extremity's brink, reducing thus
Rhyme to a kind of rope's end, a glimpsed grass
  To be snatched at as we plunge past it—
Nostalgic, after all, for a hope deferred.
  To take chances, as to make rhymes
Is human, but between chance and impenitence
  (A half-rhyme) come dance, vigilance
And circumstance (meaning all that is there
  Besides you, when you are there). And between
Rest-in-peace and precipice,
  Inertia and perversion, come the varieties
Increase, lease, re-lease (in both
  Senses); and immersion, conversion—of inert
Mass, that is, into energies to combat confusion.
  Let rhyme be my conclusion.

Painting wakes up the hand, draws-in your sense of muscular co-
ordination, your sense of the body, if you like. Poetry also, as it
pivots on its stresses, as it rides forward over the line-endings, or
comes to rest at pauses *in* the line, poetry also brings the whole
man into play and his bodily sense of himself. But there is no
near, actual equivalent in painting for tone and rhythm adjusted

by line lengths and by pauses within and at the ends of lines. There is no near equivalent because the medium is so very different. You may write with a pencil, but once you come to draw with it, what a diverse end those marks serve. But the fortuitous element is still there—the element of meeting something you didn't expect, something that isn't yourself. And once you attend to it, whatever you are starts to see an interesting challenge to its own relaxed complacency. Quite by accident you find, on a beach, the skull of a sea bird, for instance. You could put it in a cabinet or forget it in a safe place, but instead you draw it. You begin to know far more about the structure of that particular skull, as eye and pencil try to keep up with each other.

There is a lot, though, you can't know about—the mysterious darkness of its interior, the intriguing and impenetrable holes and slots where something or other has now rotted away and left a clean emptiness. The cleanliness, the natural geometry of the skull suggest the idea of surrounding it in a geometry of your own—carefully ruled lines that set off the skull, that extend it, that bed it in a universe of contrasting lines of force. Just as rhyme dancing with thought led you through to a world of human values, so skull and line build up and outwards into a containing universe.

Now, there is something very resistant about this skull. You feel you could etch a very tiny poem on it called, perhaps, 'To be Engraved on the Skull of a Cormorant'. To do so you would have to be both tough and careful with it—

> . . . as searching as the sea
> that picked and pared
> this head yet spared
> its frail acuity.

And so you go on to write a whole poem:

> *To be Engraved on the*
> *Skull of a Cormorant*
> across the thin
> façade, the galleried-
> with-membrane head:
> narrowing, to take
> the eye-dividing
> declivity where
> the beginning beak
> prepares for flight
> in a still-
> perfect salience:

here, your glass
needs must stay
steady and your gross
needle re-tip
itself with reticence
but be
as searching as the sea
that picked and pared
this head yet spared
its frail acuity.

And so a poem comes out of this find, as well as drawings. But
that interior darkness goes on bothering you. How could I relate
it, you think, to the little universe my lines netted together
around it?

This particular problem was solved by forgetting about it. Or
by seeming to forget and doing something else. Three years after
making a drawing, 'Long-beaked Skull', I did a decalcomania-col-
lage called 'The Sleep of Animals': here two skulls are filled by a
dream of the landscapes the bird and animal presences have been
moving through. The dream articulates the darkness. I try to suggest a whole world in each head. There is the hint that this sleep
is, perhaps, death in which both the head and nature are now
one.

In writing poetry, you sometimes run aground on silence, and
it takes months or sometimes years to learn what it is you wish to
say. In the meantime, you are half-consciously turning the problem over, while, at the same time, furthering the knowledge of
your medium. Among the techniques I had worked with between
'Long-beaked Skull' and 'The Sleep of Animals' were those I
have described—collage and decalcomania. I had suddenly seen
something rather like—though not yet *much* like—two skulls merged
in the landscape of my decalcomania, my chaos of crushed pigment floating in water. Instead of continuing to paint, once the
sheet had dried, I cut out the skulls with scissors, glued new
shapes on to them, then fitted them into a quite rigorous design
held together by ruled lines and called it 'The Sleep of Animals'.
I realized I had discovered a response to the dark, unenterable
interior of that first bird's skull. My response seemed to have
arrived instantaneously, but—again like poetry—the formal pattern
had taken up chance elements, had been the result of conscious
and sub-conscious processes and of that strange, unifying movement of recognition when, reaching for the scissors, what I'd

found became what I'd chosen. 'Chance' rhymed with 'dance' once more.

Why, as an artist, should one return so obsessively to the shape of the skull, whether animal or human? I do not believe that one comes back to it merely as a *memento mori*—though *that* element is present too. What seems equally important is the skull seen as a piece of architecture. It resembles a house with lit façade and shadowy interior. However much it possesses of bleak finality, it always involves one in the fascination of inside and outside, that primary lure of the human mind seeking to go beyond itself, taking purchase on the welcoming or threatening surfaces of the world, and both anxious and enriched because of the sense of what lies behind or beneath those surfaces. I tried to make this knowledge present to myself in many drawings, particularly of animal skulls. I tried, also, to articulate this knowledge with words, in the form of a poem-in-prose called *Skullshapes*.

Skulls. Finalities. They emerge towards new beginnings from undergrowth. Along with stones, fossils, flint keel-scrapers and spoke-shaves, along with bowls of clay pipes heel-stamped with their makers' marks, comes the rural detritus of cattle skulls brought home by children. They are moss-stained, filthy with soil. Washing them of their mottlings, the hand grows conscious of weight, weight sharp with jaggednesses. Suspend them from a nail and one feels the bone-clumsiness go out of them: there is weight still in their vertical pull downwards from the nail, but there is also a hanging fragility. The two qualities fuse and the brush translates this fusion as wit, where leg-like appendages conclude the skulls' dangling mass.

Shadow explores them. It sockets the eye-holes with black. It reaches like fingers into the places one cannot see. Skulls are a keen instance of this duality of the visible: it borders what the eye cannot make out, it transcends itself with the suggestion of all that is there beside what lies within the eyes' possession: it cannot be possessed. Flooded with light, the skull is at once manifest surface and labyrinth of recesses. Shadow reaches down out of this world of helmeted cavities and declares it.

One sees. But not merely the passive mirrorings of the retinal mosaic—nor, like Ruskin's blind man struck suddenly by vision, without memory or conception. The senses, reminded by other seeings, bring to bear on the act of vision their pattern of images; they give point and place to an otherwise naked and homeless impression. It is the mind sees. But what it sees consists not solely of that by which it is confronted grasped in the light of that which it remembers. It sees possibility.

The skulls of birds, hard to the touch, are delicate to the eye. Egg-like in the round of the skull itself and as if the spherical shape were the result of an act like glass-blowing, they resist the eyes' imaginings with the blade of the beak which no lyrical admiration can attenuate to frailty.

The skull of nature is recess and volume. The skull of art—of possibility—is recess, volume and also lines—lines of containment, lines of extension. In seeing, one already extends the retinal impression, searchingly and instantaneously. Brush and pen extend the search beyond the instant, touch discloses a future. Volume, knived across by the challenge of a line, the raggedness of flaking bone countered by ruled, triangular facets, a cowskull opens a visionary field, a play of universals.

In both graphic and poetic art, I like something lucid surrounded by something mysterious. I see poems and pictures as the place where the civilized, discriminating faculties and the sense of the elemental, of origins, reinforce each other. I go back, time and again, to the idea of a seascape

> with illegible depths
> and lucid passages,
> bestiary of stones,
> book without pages . . .

and a poem seems to be composing itself that could well be a picture, or several pictures:

> *On Water*
>
> 'Furrow' is inexact:
> no ship could be
> converted to a plough
> travelling this vitreous ebony:
>
> seal it in sea-caves and
> you cannot still it:
> image on image bends
> where half-lights fill it
>
> with illegible depths
> and lucid passages,
> bestiary of stones,
> book without pages:

and yet it confers
as much as it denies:
we are orphaned and fathered
by such solid vacancies:

When words seem too abstract, then I find myself painting the sea with the very thing it is composed of—water, and allowing its thinning and separation of the pigment to reveal an image of its own nature. I spoke earlier of bringing things to stand in the light of origin. When you paint with water and are painting the image of water, you return to it, as to all primal things, with a sense of recognition—water! we came from this. 'Human tears,' says the scientist, 'are a re-creation of the primordial ocean which, in the first stages of evolution, bathed the first eyes.' Perhaps the carnal echo that the contemplation of water awakens in us sounds over those immense distances of time. Or if that thought is too fanciful, when from the ruck and chaos of black paint I find myself paradoxically creating a world of water, light and air, perhaps that same chance is somewhere present in the deed, which led a boy by night along a dark canal in a blackened city and showed him fire unquenchably burning within water.

I conclude with a final poem:

At Stoke

I have lived in a single landscape. Every tone
    And turn have had for their ground
These beginnings in grey-black: a land
    Too handled to be primary—all the same,
The first in feeling. I thought it once
    Too desolate, diminished and too tame
To be the foundation for anything. It straggles
    A haggard valley and lets through
Discouraged greennesses, lights from a pond or two.
    By ash-tips, or where the streets give out
In cindery in-betweens, the hills
    Swell up and free of it to where, behind
The whole vapoury, patched battlefield,
    The cows stand steaming in an acrid wind.
This place, the first to seize on my heart and eye,
    Has been their hornbook and their history.